WALKING on a WASHING LINE

WALKING on a WASHING LINE
Poems of Kim Seung-Hee

Translated by
BROTHER ANTHONY OF TAIZÉ
LEE HYUNG-JIN

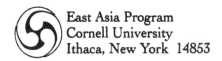
East Asia Program
Cornell University
Ithaca, New York 14853

The Cornell East Asia Series is published by the Cornell University East Asia Program (distinct from Cornell University Press). We publish books on a variety of scholarly topics relating to East Asia as a service to the academic community and the general public. Standing Orders, which provide for automatic notification and invoicing of each title in the series upon publication are accepted.

If after review by internal and external readers a manuscript is accepted for publication, it is published on the basis of camera-ready copy provided by the author who is responsible for any copyediting and manuscript formatting. Alternative arrangements should be made with approval of the Series. Address submission inquiries to CEAS Editorial Board, East Asia Program, Cornell University, Ithaca, New York 14853-7601.

The publication of this book has been made possible by generous support from the Korea Literature Translation Institute.

Number 150 in the Cornell East Asia Series
English translations copyright ©2011 by Brother Anthony of Taizé. All rights reserved. Korean original texts copyright by editors as indicated on page iv and by Kim Seung-Hee.
ISSN: 1050-2955
ISBN: 978-1-933947-20-4 hc
ISBN: 978-1-933947-50-1 pb
Library of Congress Control Number: 2010935303

24 23 22 21 20 19 18 17 16 15 14 13 12 11   9 8 7 6 5 4 3 2 1

CONTENTS

KIM SEUNG-HEE

Born in Gwangju (South Jeolla Province) in 1952, Kim Seung-Hee
(Kim Sǔng-hǔi) graduated from the English Department of Sogang
University (Seoul) before entering the Korean Department's
graduate program in the same university for her M.A. and Ph.D.
degrees. She is now a professor in the Korean Department there.
Her life as a poet began when she won the New Writers' Award
of the Gyeonghyang newspaper in 1973; in 1994 she also gained
recognition as a novelist, with the short story "On the Way to
Santa Fe." In addition to two volumes of fiction, a collection of
short stories and a novel, she has published nine volumes of poetry
(titles translated): Sun Mass (1979), Concerto for the Left Hand
(1983), Love Song for Incompletion (1987), Life in the Egg (1989),
How Shall I Get Out? (1991), The Heaviest Struggle in the World
(1995), Laughter Speeding Away on a Broomstick (2000), and
Pots Bobbing (2006). She has received several major awards,
including the 1991 Sowol Poetry Award and the 2003 Go Jeong-
Hee Literature Award. She was one of the very few women poets
to be included in the recently published *Columbia Anthology of Modern
Korean Poetry* (Columbia University Press, 2004). Her most recent
volume, Pots Bobbing, was awarded the poetry award in Korea's
2006 This Year's Art Awards. A volume of English translations of
some of her earlier poems, *I Want to Hijack an Airplane,* was published
by Homa & Sekey (New York) in 2004.

ACKNOWLEDGMENTS

The following poems were originally published in *Pich'arurŭl t'ago tallinŭn usum* (Laughter speeding away on a broomstick) (Seoul: Minŭmsa, 2000): *The Table Prepares the Rice, Love 2, Life Begins at Wounded Knee, Coughing Woman, Dreaming, The 13th Day of the 13th Month, Final Festival, Love 3, Death Korean-style, Missing Persons, Korean-style*. The last three poems listed here have been placed at the end of the present selection. They are reproduced and translated by kind permission of the publishers. The poems from *Translucent Opacity* through *Parrot Breeding* were written since 2006 and have not yet been published in a collection.

The remaining poems are from the collection *Naembinŭn tungtung* (*Pots Bobbing*) (Seoul: Ch'angbi, 2006). They are reproduced and translated by kind permission of the publishers. With the exception of *Walking on a Washing Line*, they follow the order in which they were originally published.

PREFACE

Kim Seung-Hee's poetry is usually described in Korea as "feminist," "subversive" and "surrealist." Most important is the way her poetic voices differ radically from any other Korean poet's, male or female. The distinctive energy, the rapid twists and unexpected turns of her poems have a lot to do with the way she writes. She has said that when she writes the first line of a poem, she does not know what the second line will be; each line, image or segment gives rise to what follows in a subconscious process over which she tries not to exercise control. The result clearly depends on a strong thematic unity that often springs from a deep compassion. If she is a feminist writer, it is above all in that she is strongly aware of the many ways in which women suffer simply because they are women, whether in Korea or elsewhere, and she makes that a central concern of her work. In some poems she plumbs the depths and complexity of the most intense human pain and solitude, without concern for gender. Yet she is also a very humorous poet, with a wry smile often the best and most natural response to the scenes she evokes.

Her language is direct and colloquial in ways that make translation a fascinating challenge; amazingly, her poems work effectively in English, where a lot of Korean poetry turns into flavorless mush. Indeed, it might be that her work has sometimes found a readier acceptance among readers of the English translations than among Koreans reading the originals, who are often puzzled by the seeming lack of conventional poetic themes and female sensitivity. This is in part explained by words written by the poet herself in a study of some modern Korean women poets:

"Toward the end of the 1970s, Korean feminist poetry underwent a radical change of direction. Until then, accepting traditional lyric forms, the poetry written by women had been almost entirely lyric poetry that celebrated in gentle, restrained language what might be termed 'feminine' subjects such as love, motherhood, or nature; now rejecting that, it underwent a tremendous change, moving toward feministic critical poetry and feministic confessional poetry. Among the poets writing feministic critical poems, Go Jeong-hui stands out, while among the feministic confessional poets we might include Choi Seung-ja, Kim Seung-hee, Kim Hye-sun, Kim Jeong-nan, Bak Seo-won, Seok Yeong-hui and Yi Yeon-ju.

"There are three main reasons why Korean feministic poetry turned in the direction of confessional poetry. The first was that, politically, under the political structures of authoritarianism, the three major themes known as 'anti-governmental,' 'nationalistic' and 'democratic' gained in power, and in each of those areas the individual was oppressed. Thus the confessional mode arose as a method of exploring the crisis in the meaning of the individual. Second, in literary circles, there had been conflicts in the 1960s between 'pure' and 'committed' writing, and in the 1970s between 'nationalistic' and 'populistic' writing. However, the lack of awareness of the individual, which could not be fully expressed in those terms, emerged as a confessional voice. Third, there was the impetus given by the translation and diffusion of the theories of feminism, as well as the confessional poems of Sylvia Plath and Anne Sexton. The fact that Choi Seung-ja, the major feministic confessional poet, translated *The Savage God*, a critique of confessional poetry by the English critic A. Alvarez, can also be seen as providing an important impulse, by introducing a critique of confessional poetry and a link between Sylvia Plath's poems and her suicide.

"In formal terms, the texts of Choi Seung-ja, Bak Seo-won and Yi Yeon-ju introduce a large amount of autobiographical context in stressing the voice of a first-person speaker. Using colloquialisms, they also employ vulgarities such as curses. Abolishing the lyrical forms of poetry, they evolve in the direction of prosaism and 'open form.' In terms of content, they dare to include mention of their own wounds and private lives while expressing impulsively the rage and even the madness provoked by paternalistic society and civilization. Expressions of female madness, that had not previously figured much in traditional lyric poetry, and of the death wish, were also included in feministic confessional poems, often employing dramatic expressions. Irony or paradox, parody, strategies of word play were also used boldly. As in Sylvia Plath, we find the 'father–male' of paternalistic culture depicted in terms of 'Dr. Jekyll and Mr. Hyde or of Hitler's final solution' (Bak Seo-won) while the daughter-female appears as a sacrificial victim.

"Confessional poetry is therapeutic in the sense that it plays a purifying, redeeming, transcending role. But in contrast to religious confession, which has the task of forgiving sin and bringing reconciliation with God, confessional poetry, where the individual's dark and painful wounds are expressed, may be termed a transgressive, dangerous form of writing since the author may experience social isolation and alienation as a result of it. But despite such dangers, confessional poets, rejecting civilization with its patriarchal systems, and dramatically introducing their own wounds, madness, and suffering, bring healing to the psychological crisis of the individual who endures alienation and exclusion in the modern world. In this way, by introducing frankly the female ego's crises and anger, madness, suicidal impulses, etc., and denouncing the oppressions of civilization in a male-centered society, the texts resulting from the turn toward confessional poetry among modern Korean feministic poets can be said to expand the theme of the individual poet's threatened individuality to a universal reality threatening all contemporary people."

The work of Kim Seung-Hee distinguishes itself particularly in this category of "confessional poetry" by the freedom with which it evokes multiple women's lives, by means of surrealistic glimpses of women's experiences of life (and death) in Korean society. This aspect of her writing seems to have impressed the poets who awarded Kim Seung-Hee the 2006 This Year's Art Awards, for they wrote:

Her poems show clear signs of her studies, by references to books, paintings, movies, television. Still, for that very reason her poems rarely provide knowledge as such. Rather, her poems reject with a language expressive of kicking and screaming any kind of knowledge or awareness gained through the media. While the language of her poems does not avoid images or stories, it is important to note the way it constantly strives to ensnare intellectualist notions. What she tries to express through the language she uses is the suffering that women experience. Of course, today's woman's sufferings are often directly proportional to the fervor for life and art she experiences as a woman. Moreover, with their strong musicality, her poems are readily recognizable as poetry. Certainly, the music she creates through her art is essentially composed of discord and disproportion, rather than the usual harmony and proportion. The way she makes choice of *discordia concors* is the source of her poetry's musicality and that, together with her modernity, creates the foundation for the avant-garde aesthetic she espouses.

Her poems are particularly marked by a sometimes almost frantic energy; they ask to be read at a quite breathless rate as we try to keep up with the flow, slip and shift of images. The surrealistic quality of her imagination is one of the qualities that appeals most strongly to readers in translations, since the specific qualities of the Korean language she uses cannot be preserved. Broken grammar is a characteristic of much modern Korean poetry, but she brings a quite unparalleled vivacity to her craft. Despite the presence of a considerable degree of pain in her poems, the overall effect is not gloom but cheerfulness. That, of course, is a fundamental characteristic of the Korean life experience, and of traditional Korean song.

The *Han*, the ancient inheritance of undeserved but unavoidable pain is evoked with unconquerable *Heung*, the vitality that has, in particular, enabled Korea's women to dominate all that life and men could do to them and come out on top, singing and dancing to the not-quite-bitter end. It is certainly not by chance that a number of Kim Seung-Hee's poems have religious, Christian themes worked into them, usually related to the Passion and suffering of Christ, indicating a hope that frankly challenges the pessimistic readings sometimes associated with feminist approaches to a women's life in a man's world. There is a key to this in her own story but she would certainly not wish her private life to be discussed here; the poems must stand on their own merits.

A note on this edition

A bilingual edition always invites close comparison of a translation with the original, especially by those fully competent in the source language. The translators of this volume have tried to be faithful to the Korean but they have above all tried to produce living English poems and have not felt obliged to strive for total accuracy at every point. They realize that there is no perfect translation of anything, and their main intention is that people unable to read Korean should be able to read with pleasure English poems inspired by Kim Seung-Hee's work. They beg Korean readers not to spend too much time looking for errors in the English, which surely exist, but rather to enjoy reading the original poems.

Brother Anthony

RECORD OF PREVIOUS PUBLICATIONS

Published in *Azalea* Volume 1
Harvard, Massachusetts, United States, 2007
   Santa Cello
   Pots Bobbing
   A Parcel of Eggs
   Blue 5
   The Rainbow's Promise

Published in *Damn the Caesars*
Buffalo, New York, United States, 2007
   Hotel Freedom Highway
   From Everland to Neverland
   Blue 3
   Blue 4
   A Piano on My Chest

Published in *Seam*
Cambridge, United Kingdom, 2007
   Sex and the Married Couple

Published in *Kyoto Journal*
Kyoto, Japan, 2009
   The Table Prepares the Rice
   Mister Mom
   Walking on a Washing Line

WALKING on a WASHING LINE

Poems of Kim Seung-Hee

빨랫줄 위의 산책

빨랫줄 위를 걷는 것이다,
구름 위에 걸린 빨랫줄을 걷는 심정으로,
위기를 과장하지 않으면서
위기를 미학화하는 사업에 나는 필히 골몰하고 싶다,
필생의 사업이라면 이제 그것이 대문자로 대두되는 세월
시인의 사업이라면 필경 가내 수공업 수준이겠지만
그런데 말이다, 그것이 만만치 않은 우주적인 함량을 지녔다는
것이다,
이 반달리즘 자본의 세월 속에서
못 먹고 못 입고 지지리 궁상인 극빈의 연필심처럼
앙상하게 마른 시인이라는 동물이
자기 손금을 파서 우물을 내고 그 위에 빨랫줄 같은
한 그루 몽환의 무지개를 심으면서
빨래를 미학화하고 극대화하고 있다는 것,
크리스털 워터보다도 인디언의 물 에로우 헤드보다도
더 아름다운 생수를 자기 손금에서 파내면서
그 분출로 이루어진 무지개의 빨랫줄 위를 걷고 있다는 것,
이런 것이야말로 역사적인 일이 아니냐,
안심하라, 내니 두려워 말라,
무지개 위의 구름보다도 더 우아하고 절실하게
피를 머금고 수반 위에 꽃피어난 글라디올러스,
주렁주렁 매어달린 숙명의 측량할 수 없는 홍염,
동대문 의류시장에서 장사를 하던 내 친구의
시체가 서해 바닷가 어느 모텔에서 발견된 날,
세상에 보호자가 없어도 그렇게 없어서
내가 빨랫줄에서 내려와 경찰서 안치실에까지 불려갔는데
나 캄캄한 극장에서 불이 난 것과 같았어,
허무처럼 간단한 것이 없더군, 허무처럼 간단한 것이 좋아,

그런 표정으로 구름 위에 누워 있는 그녀,
빨랫줄 위에서 왜 좀더 버티지 못했어, 왜 그렇게 추락했어,

WALKING ON A WASHING LINE

I'm walking on a washing line.
I would really like to be engrossed in the task of aestheticizing the crisis
without exaggerating the crisis,
feeling I'm walking on a washing line high above the clouds.
If that's a lifelong task, now is the time when it comes to the fore in
Capital Letters.
If that's the poet's task, although it may only be at the level of
family handicrafts,
ultimately it can include a quite significant cosmic content.
In this age of vandalistic capitalism
it means that this creature known as a poet, gaunt and withered
like the pencil-lead of dire poverty, with nothing to eat or put on,
digging a well in the lines on her palm then planting above it
a single fantasy rainbow like a clothesline,
is aestheticizing and maximizing the washing.
Drawing from her own palm spring-water more lovely
than Crystal Water or the Indians' Arrow Head Water,[1]
then walking on the clothesline-rainbow formed
as it comes gushing out must be really historic.
"Be of good cheer! It is I; do not be afraid." (Mark 6:50)
A gladiolus, lips full of blood blooming above the basin
more gracefully and urgently than even a cloud above a rainbow,
destiny's crimson flames dangling everywhere, impossible to measure,
the day my friend who worked in the East Gate clothing market[2]
was discovered dead in a motel beside the Yellow Sea,[3]
so utterly without any close family in this world
I came down off my washing line, went to the police morgue
and I felt like a fire blazing up in a darkened theater—
she lay there above the clouds with an expression that seemed to say
there's nothing as simple as nothing, things simple as nothing are good.

Why couldn't you have held on a bit longer on the washing line,
why did you fall down like that?

빨랫줄 위의 산책

울고 싶어도 울 수가 없고
날고 싶어도 날 수가 없어,

우아하게 살기로 한다,
구름 위에 걸린 빨랫줄을 걷는 심정으로,
밤마다 지하 주차장 벽에 차를 박아도
빨래를 미학화하는 사업에 나는 필히 골몰하여야한다.

Unable to cry though longing to cry.
Unable to fly though longing to fly.

I resolve to live gracefully.
Though every evening I ram the car into the walls of the
underground parking lot,
I really have to immerse myself in the task of aestheticizing the washing
feeling I'm walking on a washing line high above the clouds.

[1]Crystal Water and Arrowhead Water: Two brands of bottled water
popular in the United States. Arrowhead Water takes its name from a rock
formation close to its source in the San Bernardino Mountains, the subject
of Native American legend.
[2]East Gate clothing market: A large area close to Seoul's East Gate
(Heunginjimun), devoted to fashion and clothing.
[3] The Yellow Sea: The sea lying between Korea and China.

식탁이 밥을 차린다

식탁이 밥을 차린다
밥이 나를 먹는다
칫솔이 나를 양치질한다
거울이 나를 잡는다 그 순간 나는 극장이 되고
세미나 룸이 되고
흡혈귀의 키스가 되고
극장에서 벌어질 수 있는 여러 가지 일들이
거울이 된다
캘빈 클라인이 나를 입고
니나리치가 나를 뿌린다
CNN이 나를 시청한다
타임즈가 나를 구독한다
신발이 나를 신는다
길이 나를 걸어간다
신용 카드가 나를 소비하고
신용 카드가 나를 분실 신고한다
시계가 나를 몰아 간다 저속 기어로 혹은 고속 기어로
내 몸은 갈데까지 가보자고 한다
비타민 외판원을 나는 거절한다
낮에는 진통제를 먹고
밤에는 수면제를 먹으면 된다
부두에 서있고 싶다
다시 부두에........
시티 은행 지점장이 한강변에서 음독 자살을 하고
시력이 나쁜 나는 그 기사를 읽기 위해
신문지를 얼굴 가까이 댄다
신문지가 얼굴을 와락 잡아 당겨
내 피부에서 떨어지지 않는다
하는수없이 나는 그 신문이 된다
몸에서 활자가 벗겨지지 않는다

THE TABLE PREPARES THE RICE

The table prepares the rice.
The rice eats me.
The toothbrush brushes me.
The mirror seizes me. At that moment, I turn into a theater,
turn into a seminar room,
turn into the kiss of the vampire,
all the different things that can happen in a theater,
turn into a mirror.
Calvin Klein puts me on.
Nina Ricci sprays me on.
CNN watches me.
TIME magazine subscribes to me.
Shoes slip me on.
The street walks down me.
A credit card spends me.
A credit card reports it lost me.
A clock drives me, in low gear or high.
My body says: Let's go as far as we can.
I turn away a vitamin salesman.
I only have to take painkillers by day,
sleeping pills by night.
I want to stand on a wharf.
On a wharf again . . .
A Citibank branch manager poisoned himself beside the Han River
and in order to read the article with my bad eyesight
I bring the newspaper close to my face.
The newspaper suddenly grabs at my face
and won't let go of my skin.
I am obliged to turn into the newspaper.
The print won't come off my body.

사랑 2

맥시코인들은 말하지
우리에게 하나님은 너무 멀리 있고
미국은 너무나 가까이 있다

세상의 여자들은 말하네
우리에게 하느님은 너무 멀리 있고
남자는 너무나 가까이 있다

Love 2

Mexicans say:
God's too far away from us
while America's much too close.

All the world's women say:
God's too far away from us
while the men are much too close.

`다친 무릎`에서 시작된 인생

인디언 처녀가 뉴 멕시코 어디쯤에 있는
원주민 보호 구역에서
들판을 보며 홀로 북을 치고 있다

그 북은 내 머리 가죽으로 만든 것이다
그 북소리는 나보고 들으라고 치는 것이다
그 북소리는 나더러 죽으라고 치는 것이다

모카신을 신고 인디언 처녀는
들의 한가운데로 날아간다
바람을 타고 늑대가 온다
모래 상자가 엎질러지고
거기서부터 역사의 바깥이 시작된다
모래 상자 속에 묻혀 있던 빨간 심장이
혀를 깨물고 석류 한쪽이 깨어진 듯하다

인디언 처녀야 모래 상자를 넘어서
거기서 만나자 북을 계속 쳐다오
학살은 이미 완수되었고
다친 무릎에서 세상은 이미 시작하였으니
보호는 그렇게 옛적부터 강화된 것이다
보호 구역 안에 사는 사람들이 나날이 많아지고
보호 구역은 나날이 넓어진다
북소리는 나날이 위험해지고
나는 너를 듣고 있구나
머릿 가죽을 벗겨라 모래 상자를 엎질러라
시계를 풀러라 손목과 발을 구르며
선 댄스를 추어라 대지 어머니의 혼령을 불러내라
정수리에서부터 발가락 끝까지 내 피를 빨대로 들이켜라
다 들이키고 붉은 입술에 다알리아가 피면

LIFE BEGINS AT WOUNDED KNEE

Somewhere in New Mexico, at an Indian reservation,
all alone, an Indian woman beats a drum
as she gazes out at the prairies.

That drum is made of my scalp.
That drum is being beaten to tell me to listen.
That beaten drum tells me to die.

The Indian woman in moccasins
flies off to the middle of the prairies.
Wolves are coming, riding the wind.
Sand spills from its box
and the surface of history begins.
A red heart once buried in the box of sand
sticking its tongue out, looks like a broken piece of pomegranate.

Indian woman! Let's meet, passing beyond the box of sand.
Keep beating the drum.
The massacre is already over,
the world began at Wounded Knee.
Reservations were established long ago
and the number of people living in reservations increase every day.
Reservations expand every day.
Drumming becomes more dangerous every day.
I hear you.
Remove the scalp. Spill the sand from its box.
Take off your watch. Pounding with wrists and feet,
dance the sun dance. Set free the spirit of Mother Earth.
From the crown of the head to the tip of the toes, suck my blood
through a straw.
Finally, when a dahlia blossoms on crimson lips,
when you come riding

`다친 무릎`에서 시작된 인생

내 두 입술에 입을 맞추러 들판을 건너
네가 오면
지평선도 너를 따라 나에게 오리라

반도에서도 언제나 북소리를 듣고 있는 나
다른 북소리를 따라 가는 나
교통사고로 어젯밤 신촌 로터리에서 죽었던 나
다친 무릎에서 시작된 인생을 끌고
아직도 더듬더듬 걸어 가는 나

across the prairies to press your lips against mine,
the horizon will come following you.

I keep hearing the drumbeat, even here in Korea.
I keep following the sound of other drums.
I died last night in a traffic accident at Sinchon Rotary.
Dragging the life that began at Wounded Knee,
I go limping along.

Note: This poem is based on echoes of the phrase "Bury my heart at Wounded Knee," originally from a poem by Stephen Vincent Benet, used as the title of a 1970 book on Native American history by Dee Brown, then as the title of several popular songs.

기침하는 여자

저 여자는 말을 못하지
기침 밖에 못하는 여자
여자의 말은 모두 기침으로 환원되고
어떤 말도 말로 번역되지 않고
모든 말은 기침으로 번역되는 어떤 회의(會議) 석상

저 여자의 기침을 멈추게 하라
기침을 많이 하는 사람은 범죄자나 무신론자, 회의(懷疑)주의자들,
회의는 회의가 되고
회의는 회의가 되어
제 자리에 있는 것은 번창하고 병이 든 것은 사멸할지니

기침은 그녀의 정체성
치료받기를 거부하는 그녀의 정체성
기침이 땅 위로 분출한 뒤
한번 분출한 뒤
얼굴은 땅 속에서 요동치고 있는 용암 태동의 예감으로
웃는 듯 우는 듯 수배 당한 얼굴

COUGHING WOMAN

That woman can't speak.
She's a woman who can do nothing but cough.
Her every word is transformed into coughing;
at any meeting she attends, all her words are translated as
coughing,
not one of her words is translated as words.

Make that woman's coughing stop!
Anyone who coughs a lot is a criminal, an atheist, a skeptic.
Skepsis is sepsis
and sepsis is skepsis;
being in one's proper place is to prosper, falling sick is to die.

Coughing is her identity;
her identity refuses treatment.
Once the coughing has erupted above ground,
once it's erupted,
her face is like a face on a "Wanted" poster, maybe smiling
maybe weeping,
full of forebodings that the lava seething deep inside may come
surging up.

꿈

취직 시험을 보러 가는 꿈
하얀 테이블 위에 의사 같은 흰 가운을 걸친
면접관들이 청진기, 가위, 칼, 수술용 거즈, 피 닦는 솜,
알콜 램프 등을 앞에 놓고 앉아있는 꿈
그들 앞에서 환자가 되는 꿈

산처럼 쌓인 무슨 뼈들이 탁자 위에 잔뜩 쌓여가는 꿈
큰 뼈, 작은 뼈, 긴 뼈, 짧은 뼈, 가는 뼈, 굵은 뼈
어떤 뼈는 방의 높이 보다도 더 커서
천장을 뚫고 지붕 밖으로 불쑥 나가있는 뼈
폭포처럼 쏟아져 내리는 꿈

거인 남자의 얼굴이 뼈의 산 위에 손을 올려놓고
1억3만년 전의 공룡 뼈라고 말하는 꿈
뼈를 다 맞추어 공룡을 복원하라고 말하는 꿈
1억3천만년 전의 공룡 뼈를 혼자 복원하라고
공룡의 소멸이 나와 상관이 있다고, 있다고
말하는 꿈

끝나지 않는 꿈
매일 밤 꾸는 꿈
군주적 전능을 갖춘 이 시험관들과
청진기, 가위, 칼, 수술용 거즈, 피 닦는 솜, 알콜 램프
뼈의 산이 언제나 그대로 나를 응시하는 꿈
거울은 영상들을 비추고
그 반사는 무한히 되풀이되는 밤 은하
밧줄, 부표
꿈

DREAMING

Dreaming I'm on my way to take an employment test.
Dreaming I'm sitting facing interviewers in white gowns like doctors
who have laid out stethoscopes, scissors, scalpels, operating gauze,
cotton balls to wipe up the blood, alcohol lamps, and such like, on
a white table.
Dreaming I've become a patient before them.

Dreaming the table is piled full of bones, piled up like mountains.
Big bones, little bones, long bones, short bones, thin bones, thick bones,
some bones taller than the room
so that they pierce the ceiling and stick out above the roof.
Dreaming they all come cascading down like a waterfall.

Dreaming the face of a giant, his hand on the mountain of bones,
is saying: These are dinosaur bones from 130 million years ago.
Dreaming I'm being told to put all the bones back together again,
reconstruct the dinosaur,
told to restore a dinosaur from 130 million years ago all by myself.
Dreaming I'm being told the dinosaurs' extinction has, really,
something to do with me.

Dreaming without end.
Dreaming every night.
Dreaming those interviewers with kinglike omnipotence
and the stethoscopes, scissors, scalpels, operating gauze, cotton
balls to wipe up the blood, alcohol lamps,
that mountain of bones, are all the time just staring at me.
Mirrors reflect images
and those reflections are endlessly repeated in evening waterways,
hawsers, buoys,
dreaming.

13월 13일, 마지막 축제

그 날이 오면
더 이상 나에겐 그리움이 없으리
나의 문턱을 넘어 바다는 밀물을 데리고 들어오고
밀물을 따라 푸른 수초, 해저의 붉은 산호,
수천 마리의 검은 고래, 사랑스런 연분홍 새우와
무지개 빛 진주조개들,
흰 파도 거품이 묻은 빛나는 모래사장
나의 문턱을 넘어 바다는 밀물을 데리고 들어오고

그 날이 오면
더 이상 나에겐 꿈이 없으리
문턱을 넘어 보리밭이 들어오고
보리밭은 황토를 끌고 들어오고
황토는 어디에서 끝나는지 모를 종달새의 하늘을 불러오고
코요테와 늑대들은 부엌 식탁에 걸터앉아
남은 음식들을 은박지 종이에 싸고
욕조에서는 검은 고래가 춤추고
눈보라 천장에 가득 차
벽에 걸린 벽시계는 붕대로 두 눈이 감겨지고

그 날이 오면
나에겐 더 이상 도주(逃走)가 없으리
도주들이 나에게 산산이 들어와
나의 눈과 나의 혀와 나의 귀와 나의 입과 손가락 발가락들
집시 자루에 싸들어
바람 어깨에 둘러매고
고래들 늑대들 코요테들 보리밭들 황토들 종달새 하늘
수초들 산호들 모래밭들 진주조개들 눈보라들
일렬로 줄 같은 것은 신경도 안 쓰면서
썰물을 따라 와자지껄 떠들며 문턱을 넘어 서서

18

THE 13TH DAY OF THE 13TH MONTH, FINAL FESTIVAL

If that day ever comes
I shall have nothing left to wish for.
The sea will come in with the tide, cross my threshold,
and, following the tide, green seaweed, red coral from the sea floor,
thousands of black whales, lovely pink shrimp,
rainbow-hued mother-of-pearl shells,
sparkling sand stained by white foam from the surf.
The sea will come in with the tide, cross my threshold.

If that day ever comes
I shall have nothing left to dream of
Barley fields will come, cross my threshold,
barley fields carrying red clay.
The red clay will summon the skylark's sky, no telling where that
ends,
coyotes and wolves will sit down at the kitchen table
then wrap their leftovers in silver foil,
black whales will dance in the bathtub,
blizzards fill the ceiling.
The clock on the wall will have both eyes blindfolded.

If that day ever comes
I shall have no escape left.
Yet escapes will come rushing in on me,
they will wrap my eyes, tongue, ears, my mouth, fingers and toes
in a gipsy bag,
then strap that onto the shoulders of the wind;
a host of whales, wolves, coyotes, barley fields, red clay, larks' sky,
seaweed, corals, sand, mother-of-pearl shells, blizzards,   ·
none bothering to queue in line,
will follow the ebbing tide, cross the threshold in utter uproar . . .

갑자기 그럼에도 불구하고! 라는 말이 들렸다

폭설의 밭 속에서 살고 있는 것들!
백설을 뻗치고 올라가는 푸른 청보리들!
폭설의 밭 속에서 움직이고 있는 것들!
시퍼런 마늘과 꿈틀대는 양파들!
다른 색은 말고 그런 색들
다른 말은 말고 그런 소리들!

하루를 살더라도 그렇게
사흘이나 나흘을 살더라도 그렇게!

SUDDENLY I HEARD A VOICE SAY: "NONETHELESS!"

Things that live in fields under thick snow!
Green barley shoots that growing push up the white snow!
Things that move in fields under thick snow!
Blue-green garlic shoots, writhing leeks!
No other colors, only those colors!
No other words, only those sounds!

That's the way, though life lasts but a day.
That's the way, though life lasts just three days or four!

호텔 자유로

자유로는 이제 호텔이 되었다.
자유로에서 자유는 이렇게도 많이 밀리고 있다.
처참한 브로콜리 같은 아침의 얼굴이여.
누가 이 아침 얼굴을 이토록 뭉개어놓았나.
자유로에서 밀리는 것은 정말 자유만이 아니다.

때묻은 얼굴에 머리카락을 풀어헤친 맨발로
조그만 베개를 가슴에 안고
아가야, 아가야, 젖 줄까, 베개를 토닥이며 돌아다니던
그 미친년의 마음을 알 수 있을 것 같다.
그런 미친 그리움을 살아본 적이 있는가,
그리움이 앞으로 더 나아갈 수 없을 때
그리움이 앞으로도 뒤로도 다 막혀 있을 때
나도 얼마든지 그렇게 미칠 수 있을 것 같다

미치거나 황토 귀신이 되어서 반쯤 졸거나 반쯤 자는 길.
서울로 가는 전봉준도 그리하였으리라. 깃발은 들었고
자유는 밀리고. 황토재 떠나 황룡촌 지나
첩첩 그리움은 막혀가고. 보은 지나 금강이여.
서울로 가는 길목마다 그렇게도 어려웠으리라
자유로에 점점 떨어진 푸른 알들이여
녹두 꽃잎이여........

호텔 자유로. 인디언 담요를 몸에 두르고
스티로폼 도시락에 담긴 김밥과 샌드위치를 먹으며
그렇게도 싫어했던 실려 가는 삶에 대해
실려 갈 수밖에 없는 삶에 대해
밀려있는 자유에 대해
밀고 가는 자유에 대해.

HOTEL FREEDOM HIGHWAY

Freedom Highway's turned into a hotel now;
along Freedom Highway freedom's snarled up like this all the way.
Ghastly, early morning faces, like broccoli!
I wonder who squashed all these early-morning faces?
Freedom's not the only thing snarled up along Freedom Highway.

I feel I understand that crazy woman
wandering barefoot, disheveled hair spread over a filthy face,
hugging a tiny pillow to her breast,
patting the pillow and muttering: "Baby, baby, I'll feed you soon."
Did you ever experience that kind of crazy longing?
When longing is incapable of going any further,
when longing is snarled up, hemmed in behind and before,
I reckon I could go quite mad, too.
The road where people go crazy, or turn into ghosts from the
backwoods, half-dozing, half-asleep.

Once Jeon Bong-jun acted just the same way, heading for Seoul.
People bore flags, freedom was snarled up.
Leaving Hwangto ridge, passing Hwangryong village,
multiple longings got increasingly hedged in. Beyond Boeun, there
was the Geum River.
On their way up to Seoul, every turning was just as hard.
Green peas drifting onto Freedom Highway, green pea petals . . .

Hotel Freedom Highway. Wrapping myself in an Indian blanket,
nibbling *gimbap* and sandwiches packed in styrofoam boxes;
and as for this life I once so disliked, borne along helplessly,
as for this life that cannot help but be borne along,
as for snarled up freedom,
as for forward-thrusting freedom . . .

23

호텔 자유로

그리고 또 다시 언젠가 꽃피어날 녹두꽃에 대해
피기도 전에 공습 탄환에 스러진
카불 소녀의 녹슨 녹두 빛 눈동자에 대해………

And as for the green peas that will blossom again some day,
as for the greenish, green-pea-hued eyes of the girl in Kabul
killed in an air raid before she could bloom. . . .

Note: Jeon Bong-jun (1853–1895) was one of the leaders of the Donghak
Uprising, a peasants' revolt that started in remote southwestern rural areas
early in 1894 and won significant victories against Korean government
troops in March at Hwangto ridge and Hwangryong village. Later forces
from China and Japan joined in to suppress the uprising; the peasant armies
were gradually massacred as they made their way toward Seoul. Jeon was
executed the following year. His nickname was "Green Pea General."

산타첼로

이른 아침 신촌의 뒷골목
어젯밤이 아직 길거리에 많이 남아 있다
차도인지 모르고 차도에 웅크리고 앉아
잠을 자고 있는 하얀 풍선
어깨가 가느다랗다

누군가 질겅질겅 불어 흰 실로 간신히 매 놓은 하얀 풍선
가출한 조카가 있기에
차에서 내려 난 하얀 풍선의 몸을 마구 흔들었지
날이 밝았구나, 애야, 출근 차량이 밀리는데, 너는 이제 일어나
이 자리를 떠나야겠다;
하얀 풍선은 웅크림을 풀지 않고 차도에 계속 앉아
옆에 어젯밤의 소주병과
자그만 여행 가방을 사직서처럼 당당히 내놓고

애야, 소녀야, 얼굴을 들고 싶지 않은,
얼굴을 들어 바라보고 싶은 생각이
조금치도 들지 않는 이 개떡같은 세상,
소녀야, 집 나간 내 조카, 명주야, 응?, 명주야,

어제에서 아직도 빠져 나오지 못하여
오늘의 차도를 가로 막고 있는 저 하얀 풍선
언제 차도로 뛰어들지 모르는
속옷만 입은 저 하얀 풍선
어제 끓인 가락국수 같은 머리카락에
하염없이 꿈결 같은 햇빛이 내리고
졸려서 죽겠다는 하얀 풍선
햇빛을 꾸러 집나간 이후 만나지 못한 몇 해
이제야 햇빛으로 된 제대로의 집에서
오늘이 온지도 모르고 잠들어 있는 저 하얀 풍선

SANTA CELLO

There's a lot of last night left, scattered along the roadsides,
early in the morning in the back alleys of Shinchon.
Sitting huddled in the roadway, not realizing it's a roadway,
a white balloon is sleeping
slender-shouldered.

Someone blew that white balloon up, huff-puff, just managed to tie it with a white thread,
and, because a niece of mine ran away from home,
I got out of the car, started shaking the white balloon's body.
Look, it's daybreak, dear, the cars are lined up on their way to work,
it's time you got up, you must get out of here.
The white balloon remains huddled there, sitting on the roadway,
with last night's empty liquor bottles set down roughly beside it,
and a small traveling bag, like a letter of resignation.

Dear little girl, this shitty world where no one's willing to lift their face,
where no one has the slightest thought
of lifting their face and looking up,
dear little girl, my run-away niece, Myeong-ju, hmm? Myeong-ju?

Still unable to escape from yesterday, blocking today's roadway,
uncertain when it will leap out into the roadway
that white balloon,
dressed only in its underwear, that white balloon,
dreamlike sunlight falling absently
into hair tangled like noodles boiled yesterday,
the white balloon claims it's deadly sleepy,
and I've never seen her since she ran away to borrow some sunlight
several years ago, and now at last in a decent house composed of sunlight,
sound asleep, that white balloon, unaware that today has come . . .

냄비는 둥둥

텔레비젼 화면을 통해
아르헨티나 아, 아르헨티나가 냄비 두드리던 소리,
부에노스아이레스의 한여름 밤거리를 뒤흔들던 소리,
남녀노소 가릴 것 없이 냄비, 프라이팬, 국자, 냄비뚜껑까지
들고 나와 두드려대던 소리,
사람들이 한 목소리로 내지른 비명 소리
아르헨티나 아아
빚과 실업자, 극빈자, 점쟁이와 정신과 의사,
사망자와 부상자들, 그 한숨소리
나도 프라이팬을 들고 뛰어가 섞인 듯
입을 꽉 다문 채 몇 시간씩 은행과 직업소개소 앞에 늘어선 모습들
이런 광경 고요함

비 내리는 텔레비젼 화면을 쳐다보며
묵묵히 밥을 먹는다
다리 하나 부러진 개다리 밥상
아무도 그에 대해 말을 하지 않는다
냄비 밑바닥만 우두커니 들여다본다
냄비 안에 시래기 국, 푸르른 논과 논두렁들,
쌀이 무엇인지 아니? 신의 이빨이란다,
인간이 배가 고파 헤맬 때 신이 이빨을 뽑아
빈 논에 던져 자란 것이란다,
경련하는 밥상, 엄마의 말이 그 경련을 지긋이 누르고 있는
조용한 밥상의 시간,
비 내리는 저녁 장마,
냄비는 둥둥

POTS BOBBING

From the television,
a sound of pots being beaten in Argentina. Ah, Argentina!
A sound echoing from the midsummer night streets of
Buenos Aires
as young and old, men and women, all take to the streets
carrying pots, frying-pans, ladles, saucepan lids,
and, once outside, bang on them
while they all utter a single, united cry.
Ah, Argentina!
Debts, the unemployed, destitute people, fortune-tellers,
psychiatrists,
the dead, the wounded, all sighing together—
I feel like rushing out to join them holding a pan
at the sight of people lined up, tight-lipped, for hours on end
in front of banks and employment agencies—
the silence reigning over such scenes.

As we gaze at the fuzzy television screen
we eat in silence.
Around the dog-legged table with one broken leg
no one says anything about it.
We merely stare blankly at the bottom of the pot.
In the pot, radish-leaf soup, green paddy fields, ridges—
"Do you know what rice is? They say it's God's tooth.
Once, when people were wandering about, starving,
God pulled out a tooth, threw it into a field, it grew."
The jerking table's spasms are stilled by mother's words,
a quiet meal-table moment,
evening monsoon rains pour down,
pots bobbing. . . .

Note: The reference is to the pot-banging demonstrations that occurred in
Argentina in 2001 during an economic crisis.

110층에서 떨어지는 여자
9/11에 110층에서 떨어져 죽은 여자를 추모하며

110층 화염의 하늘에서 떨어지면서
여자는 핸드폰을 목숨처럼 껴안고
사랑했다, 사랑한다고 말하며
110층에서 떨어지는 여자는
두 신발에 오렌지 색 불이 붙은 것을 느끼면서
너를 사랑했다, 너를 사랑한다고 말하며
110층에서 떨어지는 여자는
꼭두서니 빛 불타오르는 화염으로 치마를 물들이면서
너를 사랑했으며 너를 사랑한다, 영원히 사랑한다고
말하며
110층에서 떨어지는 여자는
엉덩이를 다 먹고
허리 한복판을 너울너울 화염이 베어먹는 것을 느끼면서
110층에서 떨어지는 여자는
이 불타는 허리 이 불타는 등줄기 이 불타는 모가지
110층에서 떨어지는 여자는
누구나 자기 무덤을 만들 시간은 없지만
너를 사랑했다고 말하는 여자는
난폭한 머리카락 난폭한 두 귀가 갈기처럼 일어서는 것을 느끼며
110층에서 떨어지는 여자는
죽지마, 죽어선 안돼, 라고 연인이 말할 때
불길이 그녀의 하얀 두 손을 먹고 핸드폰을 녹여 버릴 때
그 때
바로 그 때까지
죽어선 안돼, 절대로 안돼, 라는 연인의 말이 전해진
귀 두 짝을 소중히 움켜쥔 채
110층에서 떨어진 여자는
사
랑
해
!

30

THE WOMAN FALLING FROM THE 110TH FLOOR
—in memory of a woman who died on 9/11

Falling from the blazing sky of the 110th floor
the woman clutches a phone tightly, as if it were her life,
saying: I loved you, I love you,
the woman falling from the 110th floor
feeling orange flames licking at her shoes
saying: I loved you, I love you,
the woman falling from the 110th floor,
feeling her skirt turning scarlet in the blazing flames,
saying: I loved you, I love you, I'll love you forever,
the woman falling from the 110th floor
feeling her buttocks being consumed,
the fluttering flames devouring her midriff,
the woman falling from the 110th floor,
her burning midriff, her burning back, her burning neck,
the woman falling from the 110th floor
is saying: We never have time to dig our own graves,
but I loved you,
feeling her wild hair, her wild ears, erect like a mane,
the woman falling from the 110th floor,
as her lover says: Don't die, you mustn't die,
as the flames consume her white hands, melt her phone,
then,
just then,
devoutly clutching the ears that received her lover's words:
You mustn't die, you really mustn't,
the woman who had fallen from the 110th floor:
I
love
you
!

신자유주의

돈 속에 아버지의 뼈가 보인다
돈 속에 어머니의 손톱이 보인다
돈 속에서 육친의 신체 일부를 보는 눈은
막막하다

돈 속에 아버지의 쓰러진 논두렁이 보인다
돈 속에 어머니의 파란 하지정맥류가 보인다
돈 속에서 육친의 질병을 보는 눈은
먹먹하다

자석이 자석을 끌어당기듯이
돈이 돈을 끌어당긴다
부유가 부유를 끌어당기고
병이 병을 끌어당긴다

그것이 메시지다
누가 먼저 술잔을 돌렸는지 알 수 없지만
원무를 추듯 자기들끼리 손을 잡고 빙빙 돈다
구름이 걸린 창문 하나 있는 것도 사치다

NEOLIBERALISM

In money I see father's bones.
In money I see mother's fingernails.
My eyes are bewildered,
seeing parts of my parents' bodies in money.

In money I see the crumbling ridges round father's paddy-fields.
In money I see mother's blue varicose veins.
My eyes are bewildered,
seeing my parents' diseases in money.

As magnet attracts magnet
money attracts money
wealth attracts wealth
disease attracts disease.

That's a message.
There's no telling who started passing the liquor round
but, holding hands, people turn and turn as if they're dancing.
Having one window where a cloud is hanging is such a luxury.

에버랜드에서 네버랜드로

가본 적이 있다, 에버랜드,
화사한 벚꽃이 만발하고 사슴과 사자가 놀고
딸기, 체리, 파인애플, 멜론, 복숭아, 살구, 오렌지 자두, 망고
매일매일 사랑의 기적이 일어나는 곳,
세상에서 가장 고운 아이스크림의 유지방 봉우리에서
블랙베리, 라즈베리, 블루베리, 크램베리의 젖꼭지가 살짝 솟고
푸른 색 파슬리 가루 아래 위스키 뇌관이 감추어진 곳

순식간에 만개했다
순식간에 쏟아지는
단 한 숨의 벚꽃 놀이,
창백한 핑크를 주 계열로 화이트, 옐로우, 바닐라 색 꽃잎아래서
꿈결인 듯 뜨거운 아이스크림 거품을 핥아먹는
단 한 숨의 연인들,
뜨거운 아이스크림, 혀에 닿는 순간 무너지기 시작하는
클림트의 입맞춤

뜨겁게 달군 도자기 팬 위에 지글지글 아이스크림을
구워내는 핫 플레이트나
모락모락 김을 뿜는 뜨거운 초콜레이트 위에 만년설이
곁들여진 핫 팥 아이스크림,
브랜디에 잠가 술맛이 진한 블랙 체리를
살짝 얹은 술맛의 아이스크림,
공기와 닿는 순간 단숨에 녹기 시작하는,
뜨거우며 차가우며 어딘가로 무리지어 사라진 벚꽃들의 환영

누군가 홑이불을 벗어던지고 도망간다,
나무에서 바닐라 색 홑이불들이 와아와아 떨어지고
스파게티 국수처럼 가늘게 뽑은 아이스크림 위에
화려한 각종 채색의 토핑을 얹어 주던,

FROM EVERLAND TO NEVERLAND

I've been there, to Everland,
luscious cherry trees in full bloom, deer and lions playing,
strawberry, cherry, pineapple, melon, peach, apricot, orange, plum,
mango —
a place where miracles of love occur every day,
on the loveliest butterfat ice-cream mountain in the world
nipples of blackberry, raspberry, blueberry, cranberry ooze
whisky detonators are concealed beneath green parsley powder.

They blossomed full in a flash.
They shower down in a flash,
in a momentary cherry-blossom festival,
under mainly pale pink, but also white, yellow, vanilla hued petals,
licking hot ice cream foam as if in a dream,
momentary lovers,
hot ice cream, beginning to collapse at a touch of the tongue,
Klimt's "Kiss."

Sizzling in a heated ceramic pan, ice cream
baked on a hot-plate or
perpetual snow capping steaming hot chocolate
with a garnish of hot-pot ice cream,
soaked in brandy, black-cherries tasting strongly of liquor
with a light topping of liquor-flavored ice cream,
starting to melt in a flash on touching the air, hot and cold,
ghosts of cherry-blossom, horded together, all vanished.

Someone tossed the coverlet aside and went dashing away;
vanilla-hued coverlets fall fluttering from the trees
and I can't find that store once set up beneath the cherry trees
that used to set various colorful toppings
on ice cream served in a thin stream like spaghetti.

에버랜드에서 네버랜드로

벚꽃 나무 아래 있던 그 가게를 찾을 수 없다,
아무튼 테이크아웃은 안된다고 하여
그 통유리창 외벽 안쪽에 앉아
그렇게 꿈결인 듯 혀로 핥아먹었었다,
혀에 맛있는 허무

에버랜드는 테이크 아웃이 안된다고 하여
문을 닫고 나오면 아무 것도 잡을 수 없는,
아 무아 아 무아 아무 아 무아 아무 아 무아 아무 아!
방향도 없고 안팎도 없고
시작도 끝도 없이
에버랜드~ 네버랜드~ 네버랜드~ 에버랜드~
에버랜드~ 네버랜드~ 네버랜드~ 에버랜드~
나, 거기, 가 본 적이 있다, 에버랜드

Having been told that takeouts are not allowed,
sitting behind the clifflike window pane
I licked with my tongue as if in a dream,
delicious nothings on my tongue.

Since takeouts are not allowed in Everland
once I emerge and shut the door, there's not one thing I can hold
on to,
ah, not one, one thing, not one thing not, one thing, ah!
No direction no inside no outside
no beginning no end
Everland — Neverland — Neverland — Everland
Everland — Neverland — Neverland — Everland
I, I've been there, to Everland.

Note: Everland is a large entertainment park in Yongin, to the south of
Seoul.

갈 소포

한 사람이 걸어간다
몹시 가난한 사람인가 보다
겨울 추위에도 입을 옷이 없어
넝마 위에 푸대 종이를 걸쳐 입었다

무엇을 담았던 푸대였을까
푸대 종이 걸친 등짝에 이런 글자가 인쇄되어 있다
'이 물건은 연약하니
함부로 취급하지 마십시오'

그렇게 당신은 내 앞에 놓여있다
소포로 배달된 달걀 꾸러미처럼
갈비뼈와 갈비뼈 마주치며
한 사람은 한 사람을 처음인 듯 전율한다

A PARCEL OF EGGS

Someone is walking along.
That person must be extremely poor
with no proper clothes to keep off the winter cold,
just some old paper bags covering rags.

What did those bags once contain, I wonder.
On the paper over part of the person's back, words are printed:
Fragile goods.
Handle with care.

There you are, placed before me.
Like a row of straw-packed eggs delivered as a parcel,
rib collides with rib and
one person makes the other shudder as never before.

푸른 색 2

영화배우 이은주는 어떻게 된 것일까,

한번 시도했는데 잘 죽어지지가 않아서
다시 급히 결행했다고 했는데
아주 황급하게 방문을 닫고 재실행했다고 했는데
어딘지 쓸쓸해 보이는 사람이 있는데
푸른 키 푸른 만큼 그녀도 그랬는데
돈을 많이 번다고 했는데
집은 월세 산다고 했는데
우울증이라고 했는데
크리스챤이라고 했는데
영화에 누드 씬이 많아서 수치심을 느꼈다고 했는데
~했는데 가지고는 아무 것도 알 수 없다고 했는데

어딘지 푸른색을 거느리고 있는 사람이 있다
무료한 푸른 색도 있지만
흉흉한 푸른 색도 있다
하늘만큼 키 큰 하얀 말이 훨훨 푸른색을 운반하며
날개 위에 수정 관을 싣고 손짓한다
이만 총총, 봐, 봐, 어서 날아보라고

BLUE 2

What happened to the film-star Yi Eun-ju, I wonder?

They said that after a first attempt that didn't succeed,
she took decisive action a second time.
They said she rapidly shut the door to her room, then tried again.
Some people always look melancholy somehow;
she was like that, blue as a blue height.
They said she was earning a lot.
They said she was renting a house by the month.
They said she was depressed.
They said she was a Christian.
They said she felt ashamed for playing so many nude scenes in a
movie.
They said there was no knowing in the end, nothing but "they
said."

Somewhere there's someone in charge of the color blue.
There's a dull blue
but there's also a vivid blue.
A white horse high as the sky lightly carries the color blue.
It waves, bearing on its wings a crystal coffin.
Enough, quickly, look, look, fly away, do.

Note: Yi Eun-ju (1980–2005) was an attractive and extremely popular
actress, performing in television dramas and movies, whose sudden suicide
provoked widespread grief.

푸른 색 3

한쪽 심장은 살고 싶다고 말한다
또 한쪽 심장은 살기 싫다고 말한다
절뚝거린다, 절, 뚝, 절, 뚝, 하다가
갑자기 뚝, 에서 숨이 멈추는 경우도 있다
한쪽 심장은 살고 싶다고 말하고
또 한쪽 심장은 죽고 싶다고 말한다
두 개의 잎사귀가 합쳐져 한 몸을 이루었다는 데 문제가 있다

어긋나는 고통은 생생하다,
주먹밥만한, 이 살아 꿈틀대는 피투성이 근육 덩어리를
엇갈리게 잡은 두 개의 젓가락이 마구 찔러본다,
배고픔과 목마름을 이해하는, 사랑의 결핍을 호소하는
붉은 피가 지나쳐 푸른 자주색을 발하게 된,
인간의 모든 고통이 지나치게 아로새겨져
견딜 수 없는 낙망과 두려움의 경련,
성녀 글라라의 심장엔 예수님이, 손발에 박힌 못과
옆구리에 찔린 창 자욱과 함께
가시면류관의 가시 모양까지 생생하게,
너무도 미세하게 아로새겨져 있었다,
말하자면 육체의 꿈틀대는 토굴, 매일 그 깊은 데까지 찾아갔던
눈물의 가시의 날카로운 인각,

명령하고 싶어도 명령할 수가 없다,
한쪽 심장은 아프다고 말한다
또 한쪽 심장은 안 아프다고 말한다
아파, 안 아파, 아파, 안 아파, 통일은 어렵다,
좌심방, 우심방, 좌심방, 우심방, 좌, 우, 좌, 우 하다가
불현듯 자, 에서 고개를 떨구는 경우도 있다
한쪽 심장은 좌로 가자고 말하고
또 한쪽 심장은 우로 가자고 말한다
너무 시끄러워 멈춰, 멈춰, 멈춰, 자, 자자, 이제 그만, 영영히!

BLUE 3

One side of the heart says it wants to live,
the other side says it hates being alive.
It goes pitter-pattering along, pitter, pat, pitter, pat and then
it can happen that, on a final pat, breathing stops.
One side of the heart says it wants to live,
the other side says it wants to die.
The two leaves, united, form a single body—that's the problem.

Crisscrossing pain is vivid;
two chopsticks, held crossed, stab
a bloody lump of muscle, alive and writhing, the size of a rice-ball;
scarlet blood, knowing hunger and thirst, complaining
of a shortage of love, going so far as to emit a purplish blue,
all human pains engraved there, excessive,
unbearable discouragement, spasms of dread,
Jesus' wounds engraved in Saint Claire's heart, nails in hands and
feet,
the wound left by the spear that pierced his side,
even the form of the thorns on the crown of thorns,
all engraved in such minute detail.
We might call it a carving cut by the thorns of tears
that daily go down to the depths of the flesh's writhing grottoes.

Though I want to give orders, I can't;
one side of the heart says it's in pain,
the other side says it is not.
Pain, no pain, pain, no pain, unity is difficult,
left atrium, right atrium, left atrium, right atrium, left, right, left, right
there are times when suddenly it drops its head at "le—"
One side of the heart is saying: let's go left
while the other is saying: let's go right.
It's too noisy, stop! Stop! Stop! Sleep, let's sleep, make an end of it,
for good!

푸른 색 3

일본시인 나나오 사카키)
'하루에 3킬로 40년 걸어서/사람은 지구를 일주한다//
하루에 30킬로 36년 걸어서/사람은 달에 도착한다.'
(심장의 통일을 이룬 사람)
(응? 뭐라고? 36년이라고?)

(The Japanese poet Nanao Sakaki)
"Walking 3 kilometers a day for 40 years / you circle the world once,
Walking 30 kilometers a day for 36 years / you reach the moon."
(Someone who attained the heart's unity)
(Mmm? What was that? 36 years?)

Note: Nanao Sakakai was a Japanese poet (1923–2008) whose poems caught the attention of Gary Snyder, who shared his love of the wild. He spent much of his life on the move, constantly walking from place to place.

푸른 색 4

네가 죽었다고 한다,
네가 존재해 있었는지도 몰랐는데
뉴욕의 한 아파트 출입문에 있는 전기줄에 목을 매고
네가 죽었다고 한다,

그 소식이 퍼질 무렵 길들여지지 않는 색 마티스와
불멸의 색채화가들 야수파 그림이 전시된다는 소식이 날아오고
나는 정말로 놀란다,
스물여섯, 암 세포 하나 없는 젊은 몸,
뇌혈관, 심 혈관 그 어느 것 하나도 고장난 적이 없는데
네가 대체 죽음의 잉크와 무슨 상관이란 말이냐,
어떻게 네가 내 마음의 불길한 심연을 들여다보았느냐,
내가 살아본 허공중의 황야를
머리 속에 출렁이는 독한 밤의 잉크, 그 황급한 소용돌이를 어떻게
알았느냐,
삐걱거리는 의자 위에 두 발을 디디고 허공중에 서서
줄 하나에 목을 매달고
받치고 있던 의자를 발로 차버릴 때의 가냘픈 심정,
그 몇 개의 환상 같은 번개 같은 심정,
그런 것을 왜 네가 알 필요가 있었다는 것이냐,
한 사람의 죽음은 다른 사람의 거울이기도 하다,
그런 생각을 한다

나는 안다, 그 것을, 그러나 모든 스물여섯이여,
무슨 일이 있더라도 스물여섯은
오래오래 살아라
광야의 돌무지 협곡을 고운 나체에 피가 맺히도록 기어서라도
앙리 망겐의 '아뜨리에의 집시 여인' 같은 풍만한 영광을 경험하고
아 아 아 아 머리에 불을 켜고
질경이가 질경이를 완성할 때까지 오래오래 살아라,

BLUE 4

You died, I hear.
I did not even know you existed, but
you hanged yourself from an electric wire in the entrance to a
New York apartment
and died, I hear.

As that news spread, word arrived that paintings in unusual colors
by the fauvists were being exhibited: "Matisse and the immortal
colorists."
I was truly amazed.
Twenty-six, a young body without one cancerous cell,
nothing wrong with the blood vessels of brain or heart,
what earthly connection was there between you and the dark ink
of death?
How were you able to glimpse the ominous abyss within my heart,
the desert wastes of the void I was living in?
How did you come to know the noxious evening's ink sloshing
around in my head, that turbulent whirlpool?
Stepping with both feet onto the creaking chair, standing up there
in the air, tying that cord round your neck,
your feeble feelings as you kicked the chair away,
feelings like a series of visions, or flashes of lightning.
Why did you think you had to experience such things?
One person's death is another person's mirror.
That's what I think.

I know all those things, but anyone who's twenty-six,
no matter what happens, at twenty-six
you must live for many, many more years,
even crawling along stony desert ravines, staining your lovely
nakedness with blood,
experiencing such opulent glory as Henry Manguin's "Gypsy woman
in the atelier"

푸른 색 4

너의 눈동자는 피를 흘리고 있었던 것 같다,
너의 눈동자는 흘러넘치는 색채의 격투 같은 타오르는 불을 가지고
있었다,
피와 불이 켜진 눈동자는 결코 오래 가는 법이 없다,
불은 곧 꺼지고 장미꽃잎의 향기는 즉시 소멸된다,
나다, 그날 밤 허공 위의 전기줄을 붙든 것은 나였다,
의자를 발로 찬 것도 나였다,
나는 그 날 밤 색채의 스크린을 보듯 너였던 것 같다,
그 순간 외롭지 않았을 것 같다

ahhhhh kindling a fire inside your head.
You must live for many more years, until the plantain has
completed the plantain.
It seems your eyes were bleeding,
your eyes were full of a fire blazing up like a conflict between
overflowing colors;
aflame with blood and fire, those eyes could not last long.
Fire soon goes out, the perfume of a rose petal quickly fades.
It was I who seized the electric wire up in the void that night,
I who kicked the chair away.
It's as if I was you, like watching a colorful screen that night,
so perhaps at that moment you were not lonely.

푸른 색 5
　　—어메이징 그레이스

아침에 일어나 보니
사자 아가리 속에 내 머리가 있었다
어떻게 된 것일까?
방이 사라지고 온돌이 사라지고
짐승의 부르짖는 광야 같은
붉은 사자 구강의 뼈 조직들이
눈앞에 다가오며 조여들고 있었다

사자 아가리 속에 머리를 박고 떨고 있는 나,
너무 늦은 것일까?
사자의 날 선 검 같은 이빨들이 오드득 오득
머리뼈 씹는 소리 들려오는데
'나는 개다'
'나는 새장 속에 갇힌 새다'
'본의 아니게 나는 무용지물이다'
반 고흐의 부르짖음 소리도 들려오고
피는 벌써 줄줄 새서 온 사자의 혀 밑에 낭자하고
그러나 몸이 움직여지지가 않는 것이다,
가냘픈 목소리들이 들린다
'사자 아가리 속에서 이 머리를 빼내어주시옵소서',
멀리 피츠버그에서 한 연구원의 목소리가 들려온다,
'그럼 제 인생은 이제 끝난 거네요?',

사자 아가리 안에서
새소리가 다시 들릴 것인가?
물소리가 다시 들릴 것인가?
머리에 총알이 박힌 채 그것을 모르고 13년간이나 살아온 사람이
있다,
몰랐기 때문에 가능했던 것이다,
총탄 박힌 머리로 56년간을 살아온 할아버지도 있다,
사자 아가리에 머리를 집어넣은 채
13년을, 아니 56년을 더 살아가는 지도 모른다,

50

BLUE 5
— AMAZING GRACE

I awoke one morning
to find my head caught in a lion's jaws.
How did that happen?
My room had vanished, the floor had vanished,
and the bones of the lion's scarlet mouth,
like a wilderness where wild beasts roar,
were approaching and closing right before my eyes.

There I was, my head stuck trembling in a lion's mouth —
is it too late?
I can hear the lion's teeth, like sharp swords, crunching
as they gnaw at my skull.
"I'm a dog."
"I'm a bird caught in a cage."
"I'm an unwitting good-for-nothing."
I can hear Van Gogh roaring too,
blood is already trickling down and pooling under the lion's tongue
but I am unable to move.
Faint voices ring out:
"Please remove this head from the lion's jaws."
The voice of a researcher from far-away Pittsburgh rings out:
"Is this the end of my life, then?"

Will I ever again hear bird-song
inside the lion's jaws?
Will I ever again hear the babbling of a brook?
Someone lived for 13 years unaware he had a bullet in his head.
That was possible because he did not know.
One old man even lived 56 years with a bullet in his head.
As I stuff my head into the lion's jaws
I can't tell if I'll live another 13 years or 56 years even.

푸른 색 5
─어메이징 그레이스

내가 희망을 포기한 것이지
희망이 나를 포기하는 것은 아니다,
거미가 뱀을 잡아먹고
뱀이 악어를 삼키는 날도 온다,
사자 아가리에서 머리뼈 하나 부서지지 않고
머리카락 하나 다치지 않고
내가 살아서 어메이징 그레이스를 부르는 날도 온다

Blue 5
  —*Amazing Grace*

I'm the one who gave up hope,
it's not hope that gave me up.
Days are coming when a spider will devour a snake,
a snake swallow a crocodile.
Days are coming when not one bone of my head will be broken in
the lion's jaws,
not a hair of my head will be bruised,
and I shall survive to sing "Amazing Grace."

빨강 색

빨강
펄 펄 끓는다
산불이다
홍역이다
징역이다
희망이 미처 빠져나오지 못한 판도라의 상자의 내부는
무척 소란스러웠을 거다
119다
빨강
클림트의 입맞춤 남과 여의 소용돌이
빨강
살기 위하여 필요한 몇 개의 벼락같은 환상
그 때문이다

정지

RED

Red.
It's boiling, seething.
It's a forest fire,
measles,
imprisonment.
The inside of Pandora's box that hope alone could not escape from
must have been chaotic.
It's an emergency call.
Red
vortex of male and female in Klimt's "Kiss."
Red.
The few thunderbolt-like phantasms needed to go on living.
That's why . . . .

Stop.

노랑 색

누구의 노랑색이 가장 아름다운가요,
나는 반 고호를 생각해요,
이글거려요, 출렁거려요, 소용돌이쳐요,
기다림의 속성을 그렇게 잘 보여준 화가는 없어요,
빨강보다 더 소용돌이쳐요,
하늘도 땅도 보리밭도 별빛도
다 일어서요, 만세를 불러요,
조이 투 더 월드 — 기립박수를 치기 직전이에요,
무대가 바뀌어요,
먼 호텔 욕조 안에서 헤어드라이어를 물 속에 넣고
파랑 빛 튀기는 감전으로 일렁거리며 죽어가는,
그런 여행자가 있어요,
그 때 보는 그런 노랑색이예요,
그래요, 그런 것을 가진 거예요

YELLOW

I wonder whose yellow is loveliest.
I think it's Van Gogh's.
It surges, it ripples, it whirls around.
No other artist depicts essential expectancy as well as he does.
It whirls round far more than red.
Sky, and earth, barley fields, and starlight,
all rise, all raise a cheer,
"Joy to the World" —just prior to a standing ovation.
A change of scene.
There once was a traveler
who put a hairdryer into the water in the bath in a remote hotel
and died tossing in the spreading blue electric shock.
It's the yellow seen then.
Yes, something of that kind.

평범한 달력

처음 달력이 올 때 누구나 두 손으로 공손히 받아들었을 것이다
고맙다고 고개를 숙이기도 하였을 것이다
처음에 달력은 평범한 숫자들의 나열이었을 것이다
검은 숫자와 빨간 숫자는 평범한 약정에 불과했을 것이다
평범한 숫자에서 시작된 달력은
자신도 모르는 새 운명이 되기도 하였을 것이다
기념일은 되도록 없는 것이 좋지만
운명의 기호가 차곡차곡 쌓여
운명 아닌 숫자가 차츰 줄어들기도 했을 것이다
거기서 아주 새로운 일이 벌어지기도 하였을 것이다
무덤에서 아기가 나오고
물 위의 수련들이 하얀 거북 알을 낳고
진홍 보다 더 붉은 선홍빛 죄가 흰 눈 보다 더 하얘지고
하늘의 해가 두 개 뜨고
헬리콥터가 보리밭에서 이륙하면서
결혼사진을 찍고 있던 어느 신부의 면사포를 찢고
바퀴에 휘어 감긴 면사포에 질질 끌려가다가
허공중에 목이 졸려 죽은 여자도 있었을 것이다
누군가 울면서 세례를 받고
다 있었을 것이다
평범한 달력 안에서 이루어질 수 없는 일도 없었을 것이다
이루어지지 않았던 일도 없었을 것이다
달력은 더이상 평범한 숫자가 아닐 것이다
기어코 누구에게나 평범하게 끝날 수는 없었을 것이다

AN ORDINARY CALENDAR

When the calendar first arrived
people must have accepted it politely with both hands.
Bowing, they must have said, "Thank you."
The calendar must originally have been an ordinary array of
figures.
Black numbers and red numbers would have been nothing but
ordinary promises.
The calendar that began as a set of ordinary numbers
must have turned quite unconsciously into a new destiny.
It's better to have less anniversary days but
while signs of destiny accumulate tidily
the numbers without destiny grow less.
Just then something quite new must have happened:
a child emerging from a tomb,
water lilies in a pond laying turtle eggs,
a scarlet sin, more crimson than pink, turning whiter than pure
white snow,
two suns rising in the sky,
a helicopter taking off from a barley field
catching in its blades the veil of a bride
as she was having her wedding photos taken
and dragging her upward, caught in the veil,
the girl strangling to death up there in the air,
someone weeping as they were baptized —
there must have been all that.
In an ordinary calendar there would be nothing that could not
happen.
There would be nothing that did not happen.
The calendar can no longer be a set of ordinary numbers.
Surely no one could end in an ordinary way.

바람을 잡으려고

미쳐야 보이는 것들이 있지,

생일 케이크 위에서 타오르는 촛불의 냄새 같은,
몇 개의 번개 같은,
목마를 탄 숙녀 같은,
연기 같은,
벼락 같은,
벼락 속에 터지는 설핏 장미 향기 같은

60

TRYING TO GRASP THE WIND

There are things that can only be seen if you're mad.

Like the smell of candles on a birthday cake
like a few bolts of lightning
like a matron riding a wooden horse
like smoke
like a thunderbolt
like a faint scent of roses exploding in a thunderbolt

수련

물 밑에 살고 있으니
물 위로 떠오르는 일이 여간 쉬운 일이 아니야,
몸도 무겁지만 마음이 더 무거워
그냥 물 밑에 살고 있는 것이 더 좋을 뿐이야,
그렇다고 침몰이 허용되는 것도 아니야,
허우적대다가 물을 먹고
먹은 물을 토하려면 물 위로 고개를 내밀어야 해,
오필리아, 나우지카, 키르케, 아프로디테,
다 역사상의 내 자매들,
파도 거품에서 태어났다는 것, 그게 좋은 거야,
어서 거품으로 돌아가야 할 텐데........
어떤 물밑 식물도 모두 향일성이라는 게 믿어지니?,
물을 먹는다는 것이 얼마나 힘든 일인지,
그래도 가끔 하늘을 쳐다보려고 올라와,
물 밑에 오래 살다보니 몸에서 잔뿌리가 돋아나 엉켜있어,
창백한 수련, 부레, 알아?, 부레?,
아니 부레 옥잠 말고 부레 말이야,
몸의 잔뿌리 털에서 파란 소름이 꽃피어날 때 꿈의 발진티푸스랄까,
부력은 그렇게 발진티푸스로 만들어지는 것,
어떤 진흙탕에 있을지라도
물방울들이 몸을 더럽히지 못한다는 것,
물을 먹는 일이 그렇게 힘든 일이라는 것,
물 밑에서는 물 위의 일이 잘 떠오르지 않는다는 것,
오랫동안 물 밑에 있다가 잠시 물 위로 떠오르면
모든 것이 형광등 빛처럼 부유스름 곡두 같다는 것,
블루의 여자, 생각나?
물 밑에서 한 번 몸을 역전시켰잖아,
아니 피아노의 벙어리 아다였나?
물 밑에서 어슴프레 나무들을 올려다보면거꾸로야, 천연색 사진을
현상하다가 만 것 같아,

Water lilies

It's not easy to rise above the water, for sure,
if you're living under the water,
for though bodies are heavy, hearts are heavier,
so simply living under the water is better, sure,
but it seems that submersion's not allowed either.
and after floundering about, swallowing water,
we have to push our heads up to cough swallowed water—
Ophelia, Nausikaa, Circe, Aphrodite,
all of them my sisters in history,
claimed to be born of the foam of waves—good, for sure,
we should quickly go back to being foam . . . .
and would you believe it? Every underwater plant is heliotropic!
It's hard, swallowing water,
sometimes rising for a glimpse of the sky,
and with living so long underwater, rootlets spring from our
bodies, grow tangled,
we're pale water lilies, with bladders for breathing,
no, not like water hyacinths—bladders, like frogs,
and when green gooseflesh blooms on our body's downy rootlets—
a dream's typhus fever shall we say?
the way buoyancy is produced by that typhus fever,
the way water-drops are unable to sully our bodies
no matter what kind of mud we may be submerged in,
the way swallowing water is so hard,
the way what's above the water hardly comes to mind under water,
the way everything's like a milky phantom, like fluorescent light,
if we rise above the water briefly after living long under water—
that girl in "Blue," do you remember?
didn't she reverse herself under water once?
or was it Ada, the deaf-mute in "Piano"?
If we stare up at the trees vaguely visible under water,
they're upside down, like a partly developed colored photo,

수련

가장 가느다란 것들이 가장 강건한 것들을 받쳐주고 있는데
그 위로 도전하듯이 하늘이 있고
나뭇가지가 무늬를 만들어서 무어라고 알파벳 글자처럼 얽혀
보이는데
뭐라고? 안 들려, 안 들려서,
지금 물 밑으로 다시 들어가,
그럼 다시 통화하자, 언제?, 나중에!

the slenderest things supporting the most vigorous things
with the sky above seeming to challenge them
while the branches of the trees form a pattern,
as if they're spelling something, tangled like the letters of an
alphabet,
saying what? Can't hear, can't hear, so
back we go under water.
Let's phone again. When? Later!

파세라

날 잡지마,
난 흘러갈 거야,
존 레논이 어느 날 신문을 사러 나갔다가
다시 돌아오지 못한 것처럼
파세라, 날 잡지마,
난 흘러갈 거야,

오노 요코, 당신이 누군가, 누구든지 뭐든지
번쩍이는 것은 다 당신은 오노 요코,
당신이 날 잡아도
난 흘러갈 거야,
둥근 장미 꽃잎 겹겹 따스한 신화를 감춰두고
파세라, 추운 벌판으로 신문을 사러 나가야지,

난 흘러갈 거야,
내 영혼의 블랙홀을 걸고 맹세해,
신문을 사러 나갔다가 카푸치노도 한 잔 마시고
인생은 카푸치노 같은 것, 거품이 많지만 그러나 따스한 것,
파세라, 날 잡지마,
가을은 오는데

PASSERA

Don't hold on to me.
I'll flow on and away.
Just as John Lennon went out to buy a paper one day
and never came back again,
passera, don't hold on to me
I'll flow on and away.

Yoko Ono, whoever you are, anybody, anything,
all glittering things are you, Yoko Ono,
even if you hold on to me
I'll flow on and away
hiding the warm myth of tightly clustered round rose petals
passera, I have to go out into the cold plains to buy a paper.

I'll flow on and away.
I'll pledge my soul's black hole and swear.
I'll go out to buy a paper, then drink a cappuccino,
life's like cappuccino, a lot of froth but warm nonetheless,
passera, don't hold on to me,
autumn's coming.

무지개의 약속

무지개를 보았니,
정맥이 파랗게 튀어나오고 울퉁불퉁한 두 팔을 가진
한국의 노동하는 여인들이
시퍼런 물에 공들여 세탁한 고운 천들을 걸어놓은
높은 빨랫줄이야,
거기 색색이 펄럭이는 채색 붕대들을 보았니,
심장의 유혈을 막으려고 여인들의 심장 속에 말없이 뭉쳐놓았던
몇 천 톤의 붕대들이
푸른 하늘을 배경으로 그렇게 채색층층 하늘하늘 걸려 있어,
무지개를 기억하지,
어떻게 가슴속의 붕대들이 거기까지 도달할 수 있었을까,
얼마나 많은 몇 천 톤의 여인들의 심장에서
얼마나 많은 몇 억 광년의 피 묻은 붕대들이 끌려나왔다는 것일까,
그렇게 멀리까지,
그렇게 높이까지,
아니, 더 갈 수 있었는데도
꼭 그만큼 중천에 멈추어 둥그렇게 서서
수려한 이마를 숙이고 지상을 내려다보고 있는
참 깊은 채색고운 마음 같은 눈썹

빨래가 날아가 하늘에 걸렸던 것은 날갯짓을 했던 까닭이다,
어느 날 혹은 바람이 빨래를 떨어뜨릴 수도 있었지만
떨어뜨리는 이유는 울퉁불퉁 피투성이 날갯짓을 하라는 거다,
다시 올려 색색 고운 채색으로 하늘에 심으신다는
무지개의 약속 그 때문이다

THE RAINBOW'S PROMISE

Did you see the rainbow?
It was a lofty clothesline
where Korea's laboring women,
arms knotted with bulging blue veins,
had hung lovely textiles to dry after laboriously plunging them in
dark blue dye
and did you see colored bandages flapping there, a multi-colored
arc,
several thousand tons of bandages
that had been stuffed silently into those women's hearts to staunch
their bleeding,
flimsy layer upon layer of hues hanging with the blue sky as
background,
reminding me of a rainbow.
How could those bandages inside their breasts get up there?
How many bloodied bandages were dragged, a billion light years
of them,
from so many thousand tons of women's hearts?
So very far
so very high
but even if they could have gone further
stopping there in a ring in midair like that,
deep-hued eyebrows like lovely hearts,
delicate foreheads bowed, gazing down at the world.

The washing went flying up to hang in the sky because it flapped
its wings.
Perhaps one day the wind might bring the washing down again
to make it flap its bloody, roughly bruised wings,
because of the rainbow's promise
to lift it up again and plant it in the sky with all its lovely hues.

가슴 위에 피아노

가슴 위에 얹어두기에 피아노는 조금 무겁다는 생각이 들지 않는가?,
휘황찬란한 검은 색이 위계적이라면 조금 위계적인데
법전처럼 번쩍거리면서도 움직이지 않는 피아노,
움직이지 않는 그 아래 아무튼 순장되는 사람들은 많다,

하얀 돌들이 타오르고
수증기 한 점 안 나는, 비등점을 넘은 열의 고요한 극한선상,
아즈텍의 태양 제물 피와 소금이 여자의 손금 속으로 들어가고
비등점을 넘은 하늘 푸르고 고요히 끓어
유서 한 장 날아가지 못하는 숭고한 정지,
충만의 해일이 넘실대며 꿈틀거리던 심장 꽃밭에
거의 피 한 방울 남지 않은 소진의 날,
소화 테레사 수녀가 심장병으로 쓰러졌을 때
환상을 타고 예수님이 오셨다,
잘 생긴 청년 예수, 말없이 자기 가슴으로 손을 가져가
피 흐르는 심장을 꺼내,
소화 테레사의 가슴 속에 넣어 주셨다,
보혈이 뚝뚝 흐르는 피 묻은 심장은
불같은 충동으로 서로에게 파고들었다,
말이 필요 없도록
긴밀하게 녹아들면서 두 개의 심장은 하나의 심장이 되고
두 개의 피는 하나의 피가 되고,
말이 필요 없도록
이윽고 그렇게 아름답고 풍요로운 불의 발전소가 꽃피신 것이다,

프리다 칼로의 링겔 바늘에서 뚝뚝 새고 있는 핏방울이
그녀의 멕시코 원주민 치마에 열대 꽃들을 수놓고 있을 때
처녀 프리다는 아직 한번도 낙태한 기억이 없다는 듯
그 화려한 치마폭에 뜨거운 심장 꽃송이들을 용접하고 있을 때
이윽고 그렇게
피아노
둥둥

A PIANO ON MY CHEST

Don't you think a piano is too heavy to be perched on your chest?
If its lustrous black seems deceptive, well, it might be a little
but the piano is motionless though it glistens like a legal codex
and so many people are buried alive beneath its motionless body.

White stones are ablaze, emitting not a wisp of steam
though the heat's quiet dial finger is past boiling point.
The Aztecs' offerings to the sun, blood and salt, penetrate into the
lines on a woman's palm;
well over boiling point, the sky is blue and simmers quietly,
a sublime stillness, not one dying message can go wafting off,
on a day of exhaustion when barely a drop of blood remained
in the heart's flowerbed, where abundant waves once billowed,
when Sister Teresa, Little Flower, collapsed with a heart disease
Jesus came in a vision, and that handsome young Jesus
silently put his hand into his breast,
drew out his heart dripping with blood
and placed it in Little Flower Teresa's breast;
that bloody heart dripping with his precious blood
sank into her heart with a fiery impulse;
melting so intimately that words were unnecessary
the two hearts became one heart,
the two bloods became one blood;
soon that beautiful, abundant powerhouse of fire blossomed.

When drops of blood leaking from Frida Kahlo's perfusion needle,
left tropical flowers embroidered on her Mexican Indian skirt,
when virgin Frida welded those hot heart's flowers
to her gorgeous skirt, as if she had no abortion memories,
soon, thus,
a piano
boom boom

시집가는 여자의 불

불을 갖고 시집을 왔더래,
화로에다 불을 갖고
머리에다 이고서 시집을 왔더래,
그래갖고는 불을 살르고 그랬더래
꺼뜨리면 안된다 해서
애지중지 불을 지켰는데
불이 그만 꺼져버렸더래
애지중지 불을 지켰는데
불이 그만 꺼져 버렸더래
불을 얻으러 집을 나왔더래
저, 불 좀 주세요
눈빛에서 불이 쑤욱 빠져 나갔는데
가슴에다 화로를 껴안고
저, 불 좀 주세요
화로에다 가슴을 껴안고
저 불 좀 주세요
가슴에다 화로를 껴안고
얼굴에다 화로를 껴안고 집으로 오고 있었더래
화로 안에 넘실넘실 불이 담긴 것이 너무 좋아
가슴에다 화로를 껴안고
화로에다 얼굴을 껴안고 집으로 가고 있었더래
집으로 가다가다 다 못가고
뜨거, 뜨거, 앞섶 젖가슴 허파 심장 막 타오르고
넘실넘실 그만 불에 다 먹혀버렸더래
화로도 놓치고 불도 놓쳐 그만 불을 놓친 여자가 되어
실화의 여자, 그만 한그루 불이 되어
넘실넘실 막 걸어가고 있었더래

Bride carrying fire

It's said a bride arrived in her husband's home carrying fire,
Carrying fire in a brazier
on her head, she came to her in-laws' home.
There she kindled the fire.
Lovingly she tended the fire,
having been told that it mustn't die,
yet in the end the fire went out.
Lovingly she tended the fire,
yet in the end the fire went out.
She left the house to obtain fresh fire, it's said:
Please, give me some fire.
The fire vanished from her eyes.
She held the brazier tight against her breast:
Please, give me some fire.
She held her breast tight against the brazier:
Please, given me some fire.
She held the brazier tight against her breast.
Holding the brazier tight against her face, she made her way home.
So happy to have fire wavering in the brazier,
she held the brazier tight against her breast,
holding her face tight against the brazier, she made her way home.
Homeward she went, homeward, but could not reach home.
So hot it was, so hot, the front of her dress, her breasts, lungs,
heart, all caught fire;
at last all was consumed in the wavering flames.
She dropped the brazier, dropped the fire; she became a woman
who dropped her fire,
a woman who'd lost her fire, and at last she became a single flame,
walking onward, one wavering flame, it's said.

여자의 지중해

대보름날, 걷기 시작한 것이 어떻게 한강변에 닿아 언덕에 섰다,
달은 크고 둥글고 단물에 흠뻑 취해
단 한번의 달꽃으로 피어나고 있는 중이었다,
지중해, 언제나 그 말은 꿈을 주었는데
여자의 지중해,
보름달은 그런 말을 생각나게 하였다

달의 뒷모습을 본 적이 없었는데
그 때 임종 직후 혼자 버려져 있던 그녀의,
초고속으로 졸아붙은 울퉁불퉁 검은 뒷통수가
달의 뒷모습이었을까,
지중해, 여자들이 몸 속에 하나씩 가지고 있는
지중해라는 슬픈 사랑

보름달 아래서 달집을 태우는 사람들이 있었는데
한 해의 액운을 가지고 말없이 타올라
재앙을 한 몸에 거머쥐고 홀로 떠나는 달집의 지푸라기에서
화장터에서 고독하게 타오르고 있던
시어머님의 마지막 모습이 떠올랐다

그렇게 조상들은 자손들의 달집으로 태워져야
하는 것인지도 모른다,
나도 어느, 날, 어, 느, 어, 느, 고, 유, 한, 날,
이 땅의 액운과 재앙들을 한 몸에 거머쥐며
다시는 되풀이될 수 없는 불의 춤을 그으며

A WOMAN'S MEDITERRANEAN

At full moon, a walk once started somehow stopped on a hill after
reaching the Han River.
The moon, large, round, quite drunken with sweet water
was blossoming just that once with a moon flower.
The full moon reminded me
of the Mediterranean — that name awakened dreams,
a woman's Mediterranean, her inner sea.

I've never seen the back of the moon.
But just after a woman has died, left all to herself,
might the ultrarapidly shriveling rough back of her head
be the back of the moon?
The Mediterranean, that sad love known as the Mediterranean
that every woman bears inside her body.

Under the full moon, people lit a new year's full-moon bonfire,
the whole year's misfortunes burning up without a word,
and in the fire's straw, as it vanished alone grasping calamities,
I was reminded of the last glimpse of my mother-in-law
as she burned all alone at the crematorium.

Perhaps ancestors ought to be burned as their descendants' full-
moon bonfires;
One day, one, one, peace, full, day
perhaps I too should burn up and away like a new year's bonfire,
grasping tightly all this land's misfortunes and calamities,
as the unrepeatable dance of the flames dies down.

여자의 지중해

달집인양 타서 가야하는 것인지도 모른다
달집인양 타서, 가서, 달빛의 풍요에 몸을 보태야 하는 건지도 모른다

한 방울의 눈물이 몸 안의 지중해를 일으킨다,
일렁이는 지중해는 높이 파도쳐 올라
달의 손에 닿으려고 혼신으로 물의 날개를 퍼득인다,
달은 오늘 다 되었다, 저 언덕에 이르렀다,
오늘 달은 다다, 다 왔다,
나의 지중해는 오늘 달에 닿으려고
심장의 두 꽃잎을 북으로 가득 두드리고 있다

Burning up like a bonfire, perhaps I should contribute my body to
the abundance of moonlight.

One single teardrop creates the Mediterranean in the body.
The waves of that agitated Mediterranean rise high
flapping watery wings enthusiastically, intent on touching the hand
of the moon.
Today the moon's complete. It's reached that hill.
Today the moon's full, it's all here.
My Mediterranean, eager to touch the moon today,
is pounding hard on the heart's two petals like a drum.

시베리아 폴로네이즈

신비에 가득하며
조금 어둡고
몸이 떨리는 듯한.........
쇠사슬에 묶인 채
시베리아로 유배당하며
괴로워하는.........
겨우
아무것도 아닌 것이
겨우 아무것도 아닌 것 같이
간신히

SIBERIAN POLONAISE

Full of mystery
slightly dark
body almost trembling . . .
bound in iron chains
exiled to Siberia
agonizing . . .

Merely
nothing special,
merely like nothing special,
barely

신이 감춰둔 사랑

심장은 하루 종일 일을 한다고 한다
심장이 하루 뛰는 것이
10만 8천 6백 39번이라고 한다
내뿜는 피는 하루 몇 천만 톤이나 되는지 모른다고 한다
지구에서 태양까지의 거리가 1억 4천 9백 6십만 Km인데
하루 혈액이 뛰는 거리가
2억 7천 31만 2천 Km라고 한다
지구에서 태양까지 두 번 갔다 올 거리만큼
당신의 혈액이 오늘 하루에 뛰고 있는 것이다
바로 너, 너, 너! 그대!

그렇게 당신은 파도를 뿜는다
그렇게 당신은 꺼졌다 살아난다
그렇게 당신은 달빛 아래 둥근 꽃봉오리의 속삭임이다
은환의 질주다

그대가 하는 일에 나도 참가하게 해다오
이 사업은 하느님과의 동업이다
그 속에서 나는 사랑을 발견하겠다

THE LOVE GOD HIDES

They say the heart works all day long.
Every day, the heart beats
108,639 times, they say,
while the weight of blood pumped per day may amount to some
tens of millions of tons.
From the Earth to the sun is 149,600,000 kilometers
while they say the distance run by blood each day
is 270,312,000 kilometers.
Today, in a single day, your blood runs
twice the distance, from the Earth to the sun and back.
Yes, you, you, you, it's you!

Thus you give off waves.
Thus you expire and revive.
Thus you are the whispering of round flower buds in moonlight,
the scudding of a silvery disk.

Grant me to share in the work you do.
This task is a collaboration with God.
In it I shall discover love.

미스터 엄마

어쩌다가 저렇게 망가졌을까,
이마엔 정맥이 물컹물컹 돋아나고
손등엔 모래사막을 거느린 알타이 산맥 같은 힘줄이 불끈불끈,
엄마는 왜 저렇게 험악하고 향기가 없나

흰 눈을 마구 짓밟으며
김장독을 들고 땅구덩이에 묻으러 가다 막무가내 엎어지며
진흙 속의 햇빛을 꽝꽝 밟아 급기야 때려눕히는 그녀,
난자의 아름다운 우아함이라고는 전혀 사라진........
엄마라는......

콩, 옥수수, 치즈 듬뿍, 고운 두부 그라탕 접시를 밀쳐내고
감자탕 속에 벌겋게 물든 돼지 뼈를
발라먹고 있는,
똥 묻은 환자 기저귀를 빨래 방망이로 진탕 두들겨
사방으로 똥이 튀어 날아가게 만드는,
엄마라는 이름의

미스터......
종군 기자와도 같은 하루

MISTER MOM

I wonder how she got so worn out.
The veins on her brow bulge,
tendons stick out on the backs of her hands
like the Altai Mountains jutting from a sandy desert —
why is Mom so grim and unfragrant?

Roughly trampling the white snow,
she takes a jar of winter kimchi outside to bury it in the ground,
falls flat on her face,
firmly stamps on the sunlight in the mud and finally beats it down,
the so-called graceful beauty of the ova all gone . . .
Mom . . .

Pushing aside savory gratin dishes made of soy beans, maize,
with plenty of cheese, soft bean-curd,
instead she sucks
at the crimson pork on bones from potato soup,
beats away with a laundry stick at the soiled diapers of someone
sick
making the shit fly in all directions,
that woman named Mom.

Mister . . .
her days are like those of a war correspondent.

아파트 속의 텐트

당신과 나는 아파트에 살아요
현대아파트 입주민이에요
아파트 거실에 하얀 텐트를 쳤어요
그러자 우리는 아파트 입주민인 동시에
게르의 유목민이 되었어요
말과 소, 사슴과 낙타들 속에서
―말들이 쉬도록 내버려두어라

텐트 안에 게르가 서자
작은 신전 하나와 나무를 때는 작은 난로,
야크의 털이나 말의 꼬리털,
원색의 색실과 짐승 가죽, 금속으로 치장한 화려한 말안장으로
실내 장식을 한 오밀조밀한 집이 생겼어요,
게르가 서자 초원이 생기고 보랏빛 노란빛 야생화도 꽃피고
초원이 생기자
살가죽에서 피가 숭숭 배어나올 때까지 달렸다던
몽고말들도 왔어요

오땅 오땅 호르똥 호르똥
말이나 양 같은 방목하는 짐승들을 거느리고
오땅 오땅 호르똥 호르똥
다시 한번 말을 타고 초원을 달리지요
두 개의 부싯돌은 부딪쳐야 빛이 나듯
그렇게 사랑했으면 좋겠어요
호흡하는 몸마다 바람이 부풀어
하늘까지 가는 돛이 되었으면 좋겠어요

A TENT INSIDE AN APARTMENT

You and I live in an apartment.
We inhabit Hyundai Apartments.
In the apartment's living room we set up a white tent.
Immediately, we became nomads living in a yurt
as well as being the apartment's inhabitants,
among horses and cows, deer and camels—
leave the horses alone, let them rest!

As soon as the yurt was set up, inside the tent
a home appeared, its interior elaborately decorated—
one small shrine, a little wood-burning stove,
horses' saddles embellished with metal,
yaks' wool or horse-hair
threads in primary colors, animal skins.
The ger once set up, grasslands appeared where wild flowers
bloomed violet and yellow.
The grasslands once there,
Mongolian horses arrived,
that I've heard gallop until blood oozes through their skin.

"Ottang, ottang, horuttong, horuttong,"
leading grazing herds of horses or flocks of sheep
"Ottang, ottang, horuttong, horuttong,"
leaping on horseback, we go racing over the plains.
I wish we could make love
like two flints striking together to kindle a fire.
I wish we could turn into sails rising up into the sky,
each breathing body billowing in the wind.

Note: *ottang* is Mongolian for "slowly"; *horuttong* is Mongolian for
"quickly."

85

쌩 레미 요양원

나에게는 친구도 없다,
폴 고갱 같은 잔인한 족속은 더러 있었지만
한그루의 해바라기와 불꽃처럼 타오르는 측백나무
이글거리는 황토 빛 보리밭과 까마귀,
별이 빛나는 밤이 있을 뿐 이었다,
어느 친구보다도 한번도 만난 적이 없는 오프라 윈프리가 더 가깝고
누구보다도, 그 여자,
뉴멕시코에서 혼자 살다
꽃과 죽은 소의 하얀 머리뼈, 분홍 사막 언덕을 많이 그렸던
그 여자, 누구지? 이름도 생각나지 않지만,
그 누구보다도 더 가까운,
이런 종류의 인류가 나의 친구다

엘리자베스 테일러가 소장하고 있는 '생레미 요양원의 풍경'이
1963년 소더비 경매에서
25만 7천 달러였으며 현재 1500만 달러라지만
정말 1889년 9월에서 90년 5월, 생레미에서는 무슨 일이 있었던가?
양귀비가 있는 들판에서
환각과 거듭되는 발작으로
오베르에서 권총을 가슴에 겨눌 때 누가 나를 보았던가?
'이 모든 것이 끝났으면 좋겠다'라고
나는 테오에게 말했다,
테오는 울기만 했다,
마지막 햇빛을 나는 바라보았다,
거기 있었다, 어두운 밤에 감자 먹는 사람들,
양배추와 감자가 있는 고요,
성경책이 있는 정물, 잡초를 태우고 있는 가난한 소작농,
누에넨의 어둡고 오래된 교회,
햇빛은 정말 아름답지만
이 모든 것이 어서 끝났으면 좋겠다고
나는 테오에게 말했다.

THE ASYLUM IN SAINT RÉMY

I don't have any friends.
From time to time there was a cruel clansman, such as Paul Gauguin,
but really all I had
was a sunflower, junipers rising like flames,
blazing ochre-hued wheat fields and crows,
star-bright nights.
Oprah Winfrey, whom I never met, is closer than any friend.
More than anyone—that woman,
who used to live all alone in New Mexico,
that woman who painted all those flowers, dead cows' skulls,
pink desert hills—who was she? I can't recall her name
but, closer than anyone else,
that kind of person's my friend.

The "View of the Asylum in Saint Rémy" that Elizabeth Taylor
owns
went for 257,000 dollars at Sothebys in 1963
and now it's worth 15 million dollars
but really, what happened in St. Rémy between September 1889
and May 1890?
Out in the fields with their poppies,
amidst illusions and repeated seizures,
who saw me press the revolver to my chest in Auvers?
"I wish everything were over,"
I said to Theo.
Theo only wept.
I gazed up at my last sunlight.
There it was. People eating potatoes one dark evening,
stillness with cabbage and potatoes,
still life with bible, a poor tenant farmer burning weeds,
the dark old church in Nuenen,
sunlight is truly beautiful, but
"I wish everything were over quickly,"
I said to Theo.

스트라디바리우스

스트라디바리우스가 명품이 된 이유는
17세기 어느 겨울,
그 해 겨울이 너무 추워서
오그라든 몸
강추위로 나무들의 밀도가
너무 높아져서

STRADIVARIUS

The reason why Stradivarius became such a famous brand?
One winter in the 17th century,
that winter being so very cold
that their bodies shriveled,
in the bitter cold the wood of the trees
grew very dense.

레몬즙을 쥐어짜는 시간

레몬.......이라고 말만 해도
입 안에 그득 고여 오는 연두빛나는 노란색
그렇게 향그럽고
그렇게 쏠쏠하고
그렇게 시디신.......

누구의 손이
누구의 머리에 닿아서
누구의 손이
누구의 뼈에 닿아서
누구의 손이
누구의 골수를 찔러서

세월이여, 레몬즙을 쥐어짜는 하느님,
뼈도 뼈 중에 가장 시디신 뼈,
살도 살 중에 가장 달디단 살,
피도 피 중에 가장 화려한 피
그 모든 것들을 짜내시고
저으시고 흔들어 부어
손가락 사이로 흘러넘치게 만드시는

레몬즙을 쥐어짜는 시간엔
말이 없다, 레몬-타임
두 손에 힘을 더하고 더하며
눈을 감고 조용히 기다려라, 레몬-타임
끝까지 방울방울 다 나올 때까지
-혼자 하지 마라, 레몬-타임
기다림은 하늘과의 동업이다

LEMON-JUICE SQUEEZING TIME

Lemon . . . even if you simply say it,
pooling full in the mouth, a greenish-hued yellow
so fragrant
so forlorn
so very tart . . .

someone's hand
touching someone's head
someone's hand
touching someone's bones
someone's hand
piercing someone's bones to the marrow

ah, time, God squeezing lemon-juice
the tartest bone among all bones
the sweetest flesh among all flesh
the most gorgeous blood among all blood
you press all those things,
stir, shake and pour,
making them overflow between the fingers.

At the lemon-squeezing hour
no one speaks, lemon-time,
applying more and more force to both hands
shutting your eyes, just wait quietly, lemon-time
all the way, drop by drop to the very last drop
—don't do it alone, lemon-time,
waiting is a collaboration with heaven.

수련은 누가 꽃피우나?

수련은 누가 꽃피우나?
창백한 절벽의 이슬 모은 것 같은 흰 빛 한 봉지,
처녀 수태, 신경쇠약의 새벽,
물 속에 빠져 죽은 여자들이 얼마나 많을 것인가?
침몰, 수몰........
바닷속까지 갔는데 거기 용궁이 없어서
용궁이 없어 무서워서
떠오르려고 다시 떠올라 보려고
물에 빠진 여자들의 발버둥치는 사랑이 밀어올린,

빛이 있을 동안 걸어가라고 하셔서

WHO BRINGS A WATER LILY INTO FLOWER?

Who brings a water lily into flower?
One small white pouch like the gathered dew of a pallid cliff,
virginal conception, dawning of a nervous breakdown,
how many women have fallen into water and drowned?
Immersion, submersion . . .
Sinking deep into the sea, only to find no Dragon King's Palace[1]
there
seized with fear at the lack of a Dragon Palace
trying to rise to the surface, struggling to rise again,
forced up by the writhing love of drowned women.

Walk while you still have light, He said[2]. . .

[1]Dragon King's Palace: In Korean folklore, those who drown descend to
the Palace of the Dragon King, located beneath the sea.
[2]John 12:35.

여보

사랑한다는 것
미워한다는 것
같이 살자는 것
같이 죽자는 것

손금이요
지문이다
같이 사는 동안
손금과 지문이 닮아졌네

배와 배가 만나야만 잉걸불이 탈 수 있는
배밀이 불새

DARLING!

Saying, I love you.
Saying, I hate you.
Saying, let's live together.
Saying, let's die together.

It's palm lines
and fingerprints.
While we lived together
palm lines and fingerprints grew similar.

Belly-rubbing firebird,
embers that can only burn if belly and belly meet

오른쪽 심장

어떤 선을 지나면 하나의 심장만으로는 살아갈 수가 없다,
패벽 때문이다,
심장 벽에서 부슬부슬 마른 꽃잎파리 가루들이 날리고
불나방 날개에서 오슬오슬 떨어지는 은박가루
또는 무슨 부스러기들이 좌우심방 통로를 가로 막는다,
손. 손은 참 외롭다는 생각을 한다,
육체의 본토로부터 가장 외따로 떨어져 있는 것이 손이다,
가늘어진 정맥으로 연필심 같은 피는 잘 공급되지 않는다,
본토로부터 떨어져 나와 손은 참 외롭다,
가슴을 쓸어본다,
머리카락을 넘겨본다,
허공에 공연히 휘둘러본다,
쟈스민 향기가 어디선가 무성히 익었는데
손은 외롭다, 손가락 사이로 쟈스민 향기가 건반처럼 빠져 나가고
있다,
저녁의 무게에 눌려 압축된
하나의 심장, 마른 풍금 건반을 다하여
저녁이면 풍선을 불어 본다,
얼굴이 빨개질 때까지 풍선에 입을 대고
허파 파리처럼 공기를 불어본다,
파아란 풍선이어도 좋겠다,
호박의 중심처럼 노오란 풍선이어도 좋겠다,
아니 홍시처럼 속까지 빠알간 풍선이면 더욱 좋겠다,
여러 색채의 풍선들을 거실 가득 불어서 둥둥 띄워놓고
손은 가득히 풍선 줄을 잡은 채
오른쪽 흉곽을 누르고 있다,
육체의 풍금 건반들 위로 색색의 풍선들이 너울댄다,
너울대는 그 자리 얼굴 없는 쟈스민 향기가 만개하고
십자가에서 피 흘리는 분
똑 똑 떨어지는 혈액이 번지고 번지고 또 번지고 더 번진 자리에서
풍선 줄 가득 잡은 손은
몽글몽글 피 비치는 줄탁의 고동으로 물결치고 있다……

THE RIGHT-HAND HEART

Beyond a certain point it's impossible to live with only one heart.
The reason is ruined walls.
Quivering motes of dry petals drifting from the heart's walls,
shivering silvery dust dropping from the wings of moths,
or other particles block the passages of right and left atria.
Hands, now, I think hands feel truly lonely.
The hands are surely the part of the body farthest removed from
the mainland.
The blood, like the slender lead of a pencil, does not circulate well
because of narrowed veins.
Separated from the mainland, the hands are truly lonely.
They rub the chest,
they stroke the hair,
they flail aimlessly in the air.
Somewhere a heavy jasmine fragrance has matured
but the hands are lonely.
A jasmine fragrance slips between the fingers like a keyboard.
Pressed down, compressed by the weight of the evening
one heart, having done its best with the dry organ keyboard,
blows up a balloon when evening comes.
It applies its mouth to the balloon until its face turns red
blowing in air as if it were an alveolus in a lung.
A blue balloon would do,
or a balloon orange like the flesh of a pumpkin.
But better still is a balloon red to the center, like a persimmon.
After filling the living room with blown-up balloons of many hues,
batting them around
the hands full of the balloons' strings
press against the right-hand side of the thorax.
The multi-hued balloons roll over the body's organ keyboard.
Where they roll, a faceless jasmine fragrance blossoms full
while the blood of the One bleeding on the cross
dripping, dropping, spreads, spreads and spreads
where the hands full of balloon strings
undulate to a throbbing beat, vaguely revealing blood.

암암리(暗暗裡)의 붉은 말

이봐요,
난 채식주의자예요,
난 채식주의자라고요,
채식주의자면 풀이나 처먹으며 조용히 처박혀 있으라고요?
그래요, 난 채식주의자란 말예요,
왜냐고요?
침묵이란 연필심처럼 부러지기 쉬운 거라고
사이먼 앤 가펑클이 옛날에 말했잖아요,
난 채식주의자예요,
난 채식주의자란 말예요,
당신이 뭐라 해도 난 채식주의자,
아니, 난, 어쩌면 육식주의자들의 재판에 회부된
채식주의자인 거야.
그래서 이 육식주의자들의 세상에서
아니 이 식인(食人)주의자들의 세상에서,
뭐라고요? 식인주의가 육식주의 아니예요?
그렇지 않아요? 식인이면 육식 아니예요?
네?, 뭐라고요?, 안 들려요?,
식인이면 육식주의자 아니냐고요,
네 그럴 거예요, 그래서 난 이렇게 살아요,
난, 아니, 채식주의자는 암암리에서 풀을 먹고 살아요,
나서고 싶은 생각도 없어요,
그러나 할 말은 해야겠어요, 이렇게 말을 하는 거예요,
난 채식주의자예요,
접시에 푸른 벌판이 있고
그 위에 푸른 들판이 놓이고
파아란 풀과 이슬과 푸른 잎사귀들,
아삭아삭 조금만 먹고
죄 짓지 말고 살자고
하느님이 가장 피곤한 7일째에 만든
이 망가진 도시에
탈레반은 무시로 출몰하고

RED WORDS IN SECRET

Now look!
I'm a vegetarian.
I say, I'm a vegetarian.
What? If I'm a vegetarian, I should eat up my grass and shut up?
Right, I tell you, I'm a vegetarian.
Why?
Didn't Simon and Garfunkel say back in the old days
that silence is like a pencil lead, easily broken?
I'm a vegetarian.
I say, I'm a vegetarian.
I don't care what you say, I'm a vegetarian.
Maybe a vegetarian
subjected to trial by carnivores.
So in this world of carnivores
or rather in this world of cannibals —
what did you say? Cannibals aren't carnivores?
Are they not? Aren't cannibals carnivores?
Aren't they? What did you say? You can't hear?
I asked if cannibals aren't carnivores?
Sure they are, that's why I live like this.
I, no, a vegetarian lives on grass in secret.
I have no intention of getting involved.
But I have to say what needs to be said. And I say this:
I'm a vegetarian.
In the plate there's a green plain
and on top of that a green meadow is spread,
green plants, with dew and green leaves,
I only crunch my way through a little,
I should live without committing sins.
In this ruined city,
that God made on the seventh day when he was most exhausted,
the Taliban come and go all the time

암암리(暗暗裡)의 붉은 말

아름다운 바미안 계곡의 석불들은 깨어지고
육식주의자들은 무시로 채식주의자의 푸른 접시를 깨고
이봐요, 난 당신과 다른 사람이야.
다른 사람.
같은 사람이 아니라고 해서
다 미치거나 자살할 필요는 없다고 봐요, 난.
그러니 내 접시에 총을 겨누지 말고 저 멀리 떠나줘요.
난 채식주의자란 말예요,
채석주의자라고요?, 네?, 네?, 네?

destroying the lovely carvings of Buddha in Bamiyan valley
while carnivores all the time destroy vegetarians' green plates
so look, I'm a different kind of person from you.
A different person.
There's no need for us all to go mad or kill ourselves
because we're not the same, I reckon.
So don't point your gun at my plate; go a long way away.
I tell you, I'm a vegetarian.
A vegetarian. Right? Right? Right?

부부의 성(性)

당신과 나의 성 사이에는
너무 많은 국제 정치와 사회상과 경제의 이면이 흘러가고 있다,
사랑과 성은 너무 많은 과부하를 받고 있다,
이 침대, 허공에 장칼이 드리워져
언제 몸과 몸 위로 떨어져 내릴지 모르는
이 중년의 침대
성은 단지 성일 수만은 없다

부시 대통령이 고이즈미 일본 총리와 텍사스 별장에서 만나는 사진
영변 폐연료봉 8000개의 재처리 완료 소식
이라크 아이들이 미군과 축구를 하며 웃고 있는 사진
탈레반이 파괴한 바미얀 계곡의 석불 잔해며
부동산 담보 대출 융자 이자에 상환 기간
종합소득세, 재산세, 부동산 취득세, 주민세며
내년 봄 선산 이장 문제
기타 등등 너무 많은
등등, 기타

당신과 나의 성 사이에는
너무도 많은 신자유주의적 유교적 경제적 교육적 민족적 과부하가
걸려 있다
사랑도 과부하가 걸려 있다
성이 단지 성일 수 있을 때
사랑도 사랑이 될 수 있고,
사랑이 단지 사랑일 수 있을 때
성도 성이 될 수 있고
허공에 장칼이 드리워져 언제 떨어질지 모르는
이 아슬아슬한 중년의 침대
신문지로 도배된 몸과 몸이
타임지, 뉴스위크지, USA Today로 도배된 침대 위에서
뒤척이다가 간혹 슬프게 만나기도 한다

SEX AND THE MARRIED COUPLE

In the gap between your sex and mine
too many stories are flowing away: international politics, society
affairs, the economy.
Too many overloads are bearing down on love and sex.
In this bed, a long sword suspended in the air above it
that might fall on body and body at any moment,
in this middle-aged bed,
sex cannot simply be sex.

A photo of President Bush meeting the Japanese premier Koizumi
at his Texas ranch,
a report that the reprocessing of 8,000 spent fuel rods in
Yeongpyeon is complete,
a photo of Iraqi children laughing as they play soccer with
American soldiers,
the remains of the stone Buddhas in Bamiyan valley destroyed by
the Taliban, as well as
the repayment period for interest on loans for the purchase of real
estate,
composite income tax, property tax, property acquisition tax,
residents' tax as well as
the task of relocating the family burial ground next spring
and so on, etc, too many
etc, and so on

In the gap between your sex and mine
too many overloads are suspended — ß
neo-liberal, Confucian, economic, educational, national.
Overloads are also suspended above love.
When sex is simply sex, love can be love too;
and when love is simply love, sex can just be sex.
In this perilous middle-aged bed, with a long sword suspended in
the air above it
that might fall at any moment,
body and body, covered with newspapers
on the bed, covered with TIME, Newsweek, USA Today,
after tossing and turning, sometimes sadly meet.

구름 밥상

검은 리본이 둘러쳐진 영정 사진 아래서
밥을 먹는다.
모란꽃 같은 구름이 밥상으로 내려왔다.
아니 모란꽃 같은 밥상이 구름 위로 올라갔다.
이 꽃 같은 구름 밥상,
어이, 어언, 어이, 그런 밥상.

검은 리본이 둘러 쳐진 영정 사진 아래서
밥을 먹는다.
모란꽃이 뚝뚝 지기 시작하는 밥을 먹는다.
흘러가는 밥상,
언제나 모든 밥상은 흘러가는 밥상이었다,
어이, 어언, 어이, 그런 밥상.

어느 화창한 날
어느 고유한 날
검은 리본 둘러쳐진 영정 사진이 되어
나도 식구들 밥 먹는 것을
내려다보고 있을 때.
어이, 어언, 어이 그런 날.

피란 원래 구름으로 만들어졌고
정액도 원래 구름으로 만들어졌고
달도 원래 구름으로 만들어졌고
해도 원래 구름으로 만들어졌고
태초에 구름 밥상
어이, 어언, 어이........

CLOUD TABLE

Beneath a memorial photo surrounded by black ribbon
I am eating rice.
A peony-like cloud has descended onto a table.
Or rather a peony-like table has risen onto a cloud.
This flower-like cloud table
Ah, ay, ah, such a table.

Beneath a memorial photo surrounded by black ribbon
I am eating rice.
I am eating rice where peony petals are beginning to flutter and
fall.
A table flowing away.
Every table was always a table flowing away.
Ah, ay, ah, such a table.

One balmy day
one particular day
once I have become a memorial photo surrounded by black ribbon
when I in turn am gazing down
at my family as they eat rice.
Ah, ay, ah, such a day.

Blood was originally made of clouds.
Semen was originally made of clouds.
The moon too was originally made of clouds.
The sun too was originally made of clouds.
In the beginning, a cloud table
Ah, ay, ah . . . .

법(法) 아래서

가시오
서시오
대기하시오
일단 멈춤
우회
직진
비보호 좌회전
U턴
U턴 금지

□ 속에서 사는 囚
□ 속에서 쉬는 숨

UNDER THE LAW

Go
Stop
Wait
Pause
Detour
Straight ahead
Left turn if clear
U turn
No U turn

Man in the □ dock
breath in the □ dock

물이 수증기로 바뀌는 순간

그 뜨거운 홀연
순간
그 미끄러운 순간
날씨처럼 항상 변하고 있는
천연,
어디에도 밑줄을 그을 수 없는
그 순간
아낌없는 순간
죽어도 좋은 순간

THE MOMENT WATER TURNS INTO STEAM

That hot abrupt
moment
that slippery moment
the essence
all the time changing like the weather,
that moment
with nothing we can underline
that unstinting moment
that moment, so utterly good

탱고- 프리다 칼로

나는 프리다 칼로다-
척추에 버스 철골을 끼고
전신마비 침대를 타고 나는 이 거리를 달린다,
빛이 직진하듯이-

침대는 나의 마차, 사방에 오색 꽃이 피었고
천장에는 거울이 달린 빅토리아식 침대,
덜그덕거리는 거울 속에 흔들리는 나를 보며
나는 웃음 속으로 직진한다, 빛이 직진하듯이-

달리는 과속에 거울은 깨어지고
직진하는 빛 속에 나는 프리다 칼로-
수억 개의 초현실주의자-
뉴욕 빌딩 위에 휘날리는 멕시코 치마-그러한 빛의 탱고

TANGO — FRIDA KAHLO

I'm Frida Kahlo.
Clutching a bus chassis against my spine,
I'm speeding along this road on a bed for the paralyzed,
straight ahead, like light.

The bed's my chariot. Multi-hued flowers have blossomed all
around
my Victorian-style bed with a mirror fixed to the ceiling,
and watching myself swaying in the rattling mirror
I'm moving straight ahead into the smile, straight ahead, like light.

At such excessive speed the mirror shatters
in the light moving straight ahead; I'm Frida Kahlo,
many millions of surrealists,
a Mexican skirt flapping above a New York building: that kind of
light's tango.

Note: Frida Kahlo (1907–1954) was a Mexican woman artist who
experienced a terrible traffic accident in 1925, in which many of her bones
were broken and an iron had pierced her uterus. She figures in a number of
these poems as a woman who suffered terrible pain but triumphed over it.

넝쿨 장미

말 못하는 자의 혀는 스스로 달려 나갈 수밖에 없다
타오르는 긴 혀가 유월 햇볕 아래로 달려 나가고 있다

참담하다
엇갈리다

피 점점 뇌수 햇불을 받쳐 들고 눈감고 달려가는 첩첩 도망자의 꽃

RAMBLER ROSES

The tongue of one who cannot speak is obliged to go rushing out
on its own.
A long, blazing tongue goes rushing out under June sunshine.

It's dreadful.
It's mixed up.

Blood, more and more, brains, bearing a torch, eyes closed,
a rushing fugitive's flowers, layer upon layer . . .

세상의 모든 재들

나는 존재하지 않는다-
그렇게 생각하고
아르헨티나 부에노스아이레스 쯤 가서
옷가게를 하거나 그 가게 뒷골목 같은데서
야채가게나 세탁소를 하며 살 수 있을 것 같다,
낡고 병든 페루 인들의 옷을 세탁하다가
어느 날 손님의 양복 주머니 속에서
이런 쪽지를 발견하게 될지도 모른다,
나는 존재하지 않는다-
그렇게 생각하고
안데스 산정으로 올라가서
크고 기괴한 여러 보랏빛 색깔의 감자를 키우는 인디오 여인이
되어서
불을 피운 돌덩어리 아래 감자와 양고기를 놓고
불쏘시개를 뒤적이고 있을지도 모른다,
얼굴에는 피와 불과 연기,
감자와 양고기를 다 먹고
달구어진 돌덩어리를 치울 때에
재위에 누군가의 손가락으로 쓴 글씨들을 발견하게 될지도 모른다,
나는 존재하지 않는다-
그 따끈따끈한 광야의 글씨를 가슴에 품고
거룩하게 돌 위에 엎드리면
예배는 그것으로 충분하고
세상의 모든 선이 합심하여 아주 조용한 재를 이루리라-
이만하면 잘 살았다, 휴우-
하고 말하며 온화한 재는 아주 조용히 미소 지어라

ALL THE ASHES IN THE WORLD

I do not exist—
going off to somewhere like Buenos Aires
with that thought
I reckon I could earn a living, running a clothes shop,
or keeping a vegetable stall, or a dry-cleaning store in an alley
behind such a store,
and one day, while cleaning the clothes of some old, sick Peruvians,
I might happen to find that kind of note
in a customer's suit pocket.
I do not exist—
going high up into the Andes
with that thought
I might become an Indio woman who grows large, unusual purple
potatoes.
Then, cooking potatoes and mutton in a pile of stones where I've lit
a fire
I might go rummaging in the kindling.
With blood, fire and smoke all over my face,
while clearing away the pile of heated stones
after eating all the potatoes and mutton
I might discover words written in the ash by someone's finger.
I do not exist—
prostrating myself reverently on the stones
with the wilderness's hot writing clutched to my breast
would suffice as worship,
and all the good in the world would unite to produce very quiet
ashes.
The gentle ash would smile very quietly
and sigh: I've lived a good life, all in all.

랩소디 인 블루

언젠가 나는 죽어 있다
오랫동안, 나는 죽어 있는데 익숙하다
나는 내가 있는 어디에서든
수년간 무엇에 사로잡혀 있는 동안에든
내가 죽어 있다는 데
동의한다
수천년 뒤 텍사스의 어느 사막 위에서
하늘을 바라보는 하나의 시선으로 나는 되돌아온다
나의 시선은 그 커다란 하늘과 지평의 사막에다
무궁한 랩소디 인 블루를 그린다
그러한 우울의 무궁동
수천 년 같은 랩소디 인 블루를 그려야만 할
우울과 비애가 나에게 있다고는
말할 수 없다
언젠가 나는 죽어있고
언젠가 나는 그렇게 죽어가면서 살아있다
르네 마그리트의 하늘이나
마르크 샤갈의 거꾸로 선 신부의 환상 속 기절에서나
그런 곳에서부터
갑자기 블루는 굴러 떨어지고
횡격막 아래 부상을 입은 비애의 첼로처럼
부상당한 블루를 질질 끌면서 절름대며 점(點) 점(點) 점(點)
푸른 깃털을 떨어뜨리며 둔주하는 담쟁이 덩쿨
랩소디 인 블루
블루 속에 묘혈을 점(點) 점(點) 점(點) 식목하며
진정한 시인이란 도망가는 사람이라고
진정한 사랑이란 도망뿐이었노라고
나의 가슴은 모든 어둠의 토지
빛과 나의 핏줄은 끊어지는 법이 없는 것
나의 가슴은 그렇게 모든 어둠의 토지
수천 년의 랩소디 인 블루가 끌고 가는 힘겨운 상승 완만 곡선

RHAPSODY IN BLUE

Sometimes I'm dead.
Over a long, long time, I've gotten used to being dead.
Wherever I am, and whatever I'm trapped by for years on end,
I consent
to the fact that I'm dead.
Many millennia later in some Texan desert
I'm coming back, a gaze staring up at the sky.
My gaze draws a boundless Rhapsody in Blue
across the vast sky and the horizon's desert.
I cannot say that
I possess such melancholy and grief
as would oblige me to draw such a perpetuum mobile of
melancholy,
a Rhapsody in Blue like many millennia.
Sometimes I'm dead,
and sometimes, while dying like that, I'm alive.
From René Magritte's sky or
Marc Chagall's swooning vision of an upside-down bride,
or somewhere like that
suddenly blue comes rolling down
and goes hobbling along, on and on and on,
pulling heavily at the wounded blue,
like a grief-struck cello wounded below the diaphragm,
shedding blue feathers, creepers fleeing,
Rhapsody in Blue
plants graves deep in the blue, on and on and on,
saying a true poet is someone who runs away,
true love was nothing but running away.
My breast's the land of every darkness—light and my veins never
meant to be parted—
my breast's so utterly the land of every darkness,
its sluggishly rising curve drawn along by a Rhapsody in Blue
lasting many millennia.

메두사의 여름

불꽃을 만져보지 않아도
불이 뜨거운 것은 누구나 안다.
얼음을 만져 보지 않아도
얼음이 차가운 것은 누구나 안다.

—그럼에도

불꽃이 또아리 틀고 있는 한 덩어리 얼음을 맨손으로 잡았을 때
얼음이 불꽃으로 튕겨지며 척추가 으스러지고
피와 살이 튀고
뜨거운 뱀 얼굴을 얼키설키 거느린
검은 메두사의 얼굴이 치렁치렁 눈앞으로 튀어 올랐고
순간 눈이 멀었고
몸이 굳었고

아담아, 네가 아름다운 동산의 그 사과를 땄느냐?
아니요, 저.....제가 아니고....이브가 뱀과 내통 .....
아담아, 네가 그 사과를 먹었느냐?
아니요, 저......제가 아니고...이브가
뱀의.... 빠져....사과를 먹으면 눈이 밝아.....
아담아, 네가 사과를 먹었느냐? 안 먹었느냐?
네 목을 만져보거라, 먹다가 들켜 네 목에 걸린 아담스 애플이....
아니요, 저.....그건 제가.....그게 아니고....
이브가.....이브 때문에.....이브! 이브! 이브!

보지 못하는 눈앞에
보지 못하는 음성들이 무성했고
아담아, 이리 오너라,
증거를 꺼내기 위해 아무래도 네 목뼈를 분질러 놓아야 하겠다.
오, 주여, 제발............
목뼈를 분질러서라도 사과의 증거를

MEDUSA'S SUMMER

Everyone knows that fire is hot
even without touching the flames
Everyone knows that ice is cold
even without touching ice.

—Nonetheless

When my bare hands grasped a lump of ice coiled about with
flames
the ice shattered like flame, the spine crumbled
blood and flesh splattered,
a black Medusa's head bounced up, hung suspended before the
eyes,
a seething mass of hot snakes' faces,
and suddenly eyes grew blind,
body grew rigid.

Adam, did you pick the lovely garden's apple?
No, I ... not me ... Eve, in league with the snake ...
Adam, did you eat that apple?
No, I ... not me ... Eve
succumbed ... the snake's ... if you eat the apple your eyes will open
... Adam, did you eat the apple, or did you not?
Just touch your throat. Caught eating it, Adam's apple caught in
your throat ...
No, I ... that, I ... not like that ...
Eve ... because of Eve ... Eve! Eve! Eve!

Before blind eyes
blind sound went prancing:
Adam, come here.
To get evidence I find myself obliged to break your neck.
Oh Lord, please ...
The apple's evidence, even if I have to break your neck.

흰, 펄펄, 나비

흰 펄펄 나비
비가 우거져 있다
물 속에 유리 막대를 꽂으면 막대가 휘어져 보인다
그렇게 나를 바라보면 나도 휘어져 보일 거다
흰
펄펄
나비
나 그렇게 비를 맞고 있어
나비,
나, 비,
젖은 신문지 같은
날개 한 쌍으로 휘어진 세상 들고
빗속에
흰
펄펄
나비,
나, 비.
무지개 구렁이 같은
징그럽게
아름다운
흰
펄펄
피안
피, 안.

BENT, FLUTTERING BUTTERFLY

Bent, fluttering butterfly,
rain's so plentiful.
If you insert a glass wand into water the rod looks bent.
So if you look up at me like that, I'll look bent.
Bent
fluttering
butterfly
I'm so soaked through with rain
butterfly
butter, fly,
bearing a bent world on wings
like wet newspaper
in the rain
bent
fluttering
butterfly
butter, fly,
creepily
beautiful
like a rainbow boa constrictor
bent
fluttering
nirvana
nir, vana.

나는 그렇게 들었다

이 운동화의 얼룩이 아무래도 지워지지 않는다,
아들은 열 다섯 살,
아무리 문질러도 지워지지 않을 얼룩을 막 묻히고 다닐 때다,
표백제에 담가 놓고 잠시 목욕탕 타일 벽에 이마를 댄다,
운동화라니, 이만한 크기의 운동화라니,
들길에 떨어진 그런 운동화를 본 적이 있다

효순과 미선은 그 날 들길을 걷고 있었다
학교가 끝나고 집에 가는 길이었다
들길 가에는 질경이, 명아주, 미나리 냉냉이, 돼지감자 풀꽃들이
희고 노오랗게 피어 있었고,
효순과 미선은 들꽃을 보며 길을 걷고 있었다,
파란 하늘 아래 하이얀 구름, 사랑이 그렇게
막 움터 오르려는 봉긋한 젖가슴
미 2사단 소속 운전자 워커 마크 병장은
장갑차를 몰며 경기도 양주군 광적면 56번 지방도로를
가고 있었다,
오른쪽 시야가 제한되어 있었고
커브 길을 돈 뒤 선임 탑승자가 소녀들을 발견하고
경고 무전을 보냈으나 듣지 못하였다,
편도 너비 3.7m에서 너비 3.65m의 장갑차를
운행했던 지휘 체계의 실수를 인정은 했다,
비극적인 사고였다,
맥도널드 참모장은 그렇게 말했다,
한미 합동 조사 결과 누구에게도 과실을 물을 수 없다고
미 2사단 공보실장 브라이언 메이커 소령은 말했다,
수사는 종결되었다고
미 2사단 채양도 공보관은 말했다

THAT'S WHAT I HEARD

I can't get rid of the stain on this sneaker, no matter what.
My son's fifteen,
all the time picking up stains that can't be erased by any amount of
scrubbing.
I rest my brow briefly against the bathroom's tiled wall,
holding a sneaker soaked in bleach.
A sneaker? A sneaker this size?
Once before I saw just such a sneaker; it was lying on a meadow path.

Hyosun and Misun were walking along a meadow path that day,
on their way home after school.
Along the path-side flowering weeds — wild plantain, goosefoot,
dropwort, sunroot —
were blossoming white or yellow.
Hyosun and Misun were walking along looking at the flowers.
White clouds beneath a clear blue sky — love
was about to bud in their swelling breasts.
US 2nd Infantry Division Sergeant Mark Walker was driving
an armored vehicle down country road 56 in Gwangjeok-myeon
in Yangju County, Gyeonggi Province.
His view to the right was restricted
so the vehicle's commander, spotting the girls after rounding a curve,
warned him by radio but he didn't hear.
They admitted it had been an error to drive a vehicle 3.65 meters wide
down a road only 3.7 meters wide.
It was a tragic accident.
So said Chief of Staff John Macdonald.
The joint Korean-American investigation team was unable to fix
the blame on anyone.
So said Major Brian Maka, 2nd Infantry Division's chief press
officer.
The investigation was closed,
said Chae Yang-do, press officer for the 2nd Infantry Division.

나는 그렇게 들었다

나는 그렇게 들었다,
켐프 레드클라우드여,
이 소녀들은 들길 위에 선명한 핏자국과 오른쪽
운동화 한 짝을 남겼다,
그리고 6월 15일 벽제 화장터에서 한 줌의 재가 되었다,
나는 그렇게 들었다

목욕탕 타일 벽에 이마를 묻고
표백제에 아무리 담가놓아도
지워지지 않는 운동화 얼룩에 대하여
떨칠 수 없는 역사에 대하여 생각한다,
처음엔 붉으스레했던 것이 차츰 푸르스레해졌는데
신생아 아들 엉덩이에 퍼져있던 몽고반점 같다고
어쩐지 그런 생각이 떨쳐지지 않아
차가운 타일 벽에 이마를 묻으며
희망이라는 것이 병이 될 수 있는 나라도 있느냐고
쾅쾅 나는 그렇게 들었다.

That's what I heard

That's what I heard.
Camp Redcloud!
Those girls left behind clear bloodstains and one
right foot sneaker on the meadow path.
On June 15 they became a handful of ashes at Byeokje
crematorium.
That's what I heard.

As I rest my brow against the bathroom's tiled wall
I reflect about the stain on the sneaker that refuses to budge
no matter how long I soak it in bleach,
about history that cannot be shaken off.
First it was reddish then it turned bluish,
rather like the Mongolian spot on a newly born son's bottom —
for some reason I can't shake off that thought
as I rest my brow against the cold tiled wall.
Is there a land where hope too can become a disease?
That's what I heard ringing loud and clear.

Note: Hyosun and Misun: two Korean middle-school girls who were killed
by an American armored personnel carrier in June 2002. The American
military badly mishandled their response and this provoked a groundswell
of popular anti-American sentiment expressed in long-lasting candlelight
demonstrations.

빨래집게

해양성 기후로 변한 듯 투명한 봄 날 오전.
죄도, 죄지은 자도 모두 외출나간 것 같은.

마당에 널린 빨래들에 관해 잠깐 바라보았다.
빨래집게에 죽어라 매달려
이빨 없는 입으로 햇빛을 먹어라-포만하고 있는 저 빨래들
빨래집게에서 떠날 수는 없다
빨래집게 더러 떠나라고 할 수도 없다
빨래집게에서 떨어뜨리면 더 큰 일 날 것 같다
저 빨랫줄과 빨래집게의 관계
저 빨래집게와 빨래의 위험한 양상

거기에 네 팔이 하나 떨어져 있다.

CLOTHES PEGS

A spring morning so limpid it seemed we'd changed to an ocean
climate.
Sins and sinners, all apparently gone off somewhere.

I glanced out at the washing hanging in the yard.
Desperately clinging to clothes pegs
eating sunshine with toothless mouths, the washing, stuffed full,
can't get away from the clothes pegs,
can't tell the clothes pegs to get away, either,
and it would be worse still if the clothes fell from the pegs.
The relationship of clothes pegs and washing-line,
the dangerous condition of clothes pegs and washing.

There, one of your arms has fallen off.

논 거울

길을 잘못 들었을 뿐만 아니라 운전까지 잘못하여
논두렁 속으로 한쪽 차바퀴가 빠지고 말았다.
어젯밤 내린 폭우 탓으로
논두렁은 강철처럼 미끈미끈하였다.
논두렁에 처박힌 차바퀴를 끌어내려고
바퀴를 들어올리다가
발을 헛디디는, 아니 그 미끌미끌한 그 놈의 진흙 때문에,
논두렁 속으로 온몸이 처박히고 말았다.
원하지도 않았는데 흙 속에 얼굴을 파묻었네.

미친 것처럼 항의하며 일어나려는데
미끌미끌한 논두렁 아래 진흙 때문에
다시 한번 논 속으로 얼굴을 파묻으며 엎어지게 되었다.
몸에 진흙이 묻는 게 싫었는데
얼굴에 진흙이 묻는 건 죽기 보다 더 싫었고
왜 그렇게 진흙을 무서워하는 건가.
이마와 콧등과 입에 진흙을 바른 채 눈을 뜨며 고개를 들었을 때
물끄러미 논물을 들여다보는 눈동자가 보였네.
고요한 눈동자. 외국인 보다 더 낯선 진흙빛 눈동자.
논물 속으로는 외국 같은 하늘이 흐르고
논물 속으로는 외국 같은 구름이 흐르고
논물 속으로는 하나의 얼굴, 푸른 어린 벼들 사이,
진흙빛 이방의 얼굴이 하나 떠있었네.

이 진흙빛 얼굴,
선악과를 따먹기 이전의
진흙빛 얼굴을 논물 속으로부터
고요히 건져 올리고 있는.........

RICE FIELD MIRROR

Not content with taking a wrong turn, I was driving badly too,
so that one wheel got stuck in a rice field embankment.
Because of the previous night's downpour
the embankment was slippery as steel.
Intending to haul out the wheel, that was stuck deep in the
embankment,
I made a false step as I pulled the wheel upward,
no, I ended up entirely sunk in the embankment
because of that wretched slippery mud.
Against my wishes, my face was plunged into the mud.

I tried to get up, protesting like crazy,
but because of the slippery mud below the embankment,
I fell sprawling once more, plunging my face into the rice field.
I detest having my body covered in mud,
having my face smeared with mud is worse than death.
Why am I so afraid of mud, I wonder?
With mud spread over forehead, nose and mouth,
as I opened my eyes and raised my head
I glimpsed a blankly staring eye in the rice field water,
a calm eye, mud-colored, stranger than any foreigner's.
In the water of the rice field a sky like a foreign land was flowing.
In the water of the rice field a cloud like a foreign land was
flowing.
In the water of the rice field, between the young rice shoots.
A face, a mud-colored stranger's face was floating.

Quietly lifting
out of the rice field's water
this mud-colored face
from a time before the forbidden fruit was eaten . . .

결혼식 차와 장례식 차

질주하는 자유로다.
나의 자유가 이렇게 존중되는 날이 있다니.
푸른 하늘 아래 글썽이도록 벅찬 이 자유!

빨간 풍선 파란 풍선 노란 풍선들을 매달고
하얀 결혼식 자동차 한 대가 앞으로 끼어든다.
질주하는 자동차 앞뒤로
색색의 풍선들이 빗발치듯 손을 흔들며
..........공항으로 도망 중이다.
매달린 깡통들이
푸른 바람 속에서 손뼉을 치며
불현듯 눈앞에서 쏜살같이 사라진다.
.........도망 중. 그렇게 도망 중.

하얀 바탕에 검은 줄을 친 장의차 한 대가
옆 차선을 달리다 갑자기 내 앞으로 끼어든다.
끼어들기를 하는 장의차는 처음 보았다,
아니 장의차는 항상 끼어들기를 하는 차인지도 모른다.
하얗고 노란 국화꽃 화환들이
유족들의 눈동자처럼 나를 빤히 내려다본다.
그 눈길을 생각하고 있는데
어디선가 파란 풍선 빨간 풍선 노란 풍선들을 매달고
하얀 결혼식 자동차 한 대가 또 앞으로 끼어든다.

장의차, 결혼식 차, 내 차-
이런 순으로 한참을 달리는가 했더니
어느 새 검은 바탕에 하얀 줄을 친
장의차 한 대가
결혼식 차와 내 차 사이로 또 끼어든다.
이제 결혼식 차, 장의차, 내 차 이런 순으로 잠시 달리다가
금새 뒤죽박죽이 되어
누가 누구 차를 추월했는지
누가 누구 차를 따라 가는 것인지.........
 자기 차선만 바라보면서 꾸준히 가도록 한다.

WEDDING LIMOUSINES AND FUNERAL LIMOUSINES

Freedom Highway goes speeding along.
To think there's a day my freedom is respected this highly.
Below the blue sky, a freedom so great it makes me cry.

A white wedding limousine cuts in front of me,
decorated with red balloons, blue balloons, yellow balloons.
Clusters of colored balloons are waving
on the front and back of the speeding vehicle
... they're escaping to the airport.
With cans dangling behind
clapping hands in the blue wind,
it abruptly vanishes from sight.
... Escaping. Escaping just like that.

A white funeral limousine with a black stripe,
speeding along in the next lane, suddenly cuts in front of me.
It's the first time I ever saw a hearse cutting in.
Maybe hearses are always supposed to cut in.
Wreaths of white and yellow chrysanthemums
stare down at me like the eyes of mourners.
Just as I am pondering that gaze
another white wedding limousine
decorated with blue balloons, red balloons, yellow balloons,
appears from somewhere and cuts in front of me again.

Hearse, wedding limousine, my car ...
After speeding along in that order for a while
suddenly another funeral limousine,
black this time, with a white stripe,
cuts in-between the wedding limousine and mine.
As we speed on, wedding limousine, hearse, my car,
suddenly it's quite unclear
which car is overtaking which,
which car is following which ...
so they speed along, each only intent on its own lane.

결혼식 차와 장례식 차

하나의 결혼식이 많은 장의차를 낳는지
하나의 장의차가 많은 결혼식을 낳는지
앞서거니 뒤서거니
그렇게도 끼어들기가 출몰하며 도망하는 자유로 풍경.

Either one wedding produces a lot of funeral limousines
or one funeral limousine produces many weddings.
Behind and before,
all escaping, cutting in again and again, a scene on Freedom
Highway.

Note: Freedom Highway is a highway along the north bank of the Han
River leading out of Seoul toward the West and on as far as the demilitarized
zone (DMZ).

뚱뚱한 모나리자

어마어마한 살덩어리
막을 수 없는 중식의 반죽덩어리
물 속에서 퉁퉁 불은 듯한
부풀어 오른 얼굴에 손가락을 넣어봐
밀가루의 무저갱으로 아득히 빨려 들어가는 손가락
야식증후군일거야
몽유의 발걸음은 냉장고 속으로 출렁출렁 빨려 들어가고
해적선, 밤의 약탈로 메꾸어지는 입,
통 닭 한 마리를 밤에 혼자 다 먹었다니까
먹은 기억은 못하지만, 아침에 쟁반에 수북한 닭뼈들,
그것과 출렁거리는 뱃살만이 유일한 증거,
낮이면 하얀 실크에 십자수를 놓는 얌전한 수예가인지도 몰라
한밤중엔 머리를 풀고 먹을 것을 찾아다니는 폭식증의 여자
미소, 어두운 심해의 우울증에서 뻗어 나오는 방만한 미소,
무시무시한 살덩어리가 움직이는 출렁거리는 비만의 미소,
몸을 증오하고 먹음직스런 세상의 모든 것을 증오해야 하는,
파묻히고 싶은, 매몰의 죽음충동을 일으키는,
뚱뚱한 여인의 환상의 끝은
매몰,
함께 죽자고 할 수는 없을 거야,
함께 죽을 순 없을 거야,
뚱뚱한 매몰의 끝은 천국인지, 지옥인지,
나는 숨쉬고 싶다,
뚱뚱한 턱과 산맥만큼 부풀어 오른 가슴에 파묻혀
숨이 턱 밑까지 차오르고 다리가 후들거리는 모나리자,
야식증의 어마어마한 모나리자,
간신히 숨쉬는 모나리자

비만 진료소 벤치에 앉아있는 미소의 어머니

FAT MONA LISA

One colossal mound of flesh,
a lump of dough, expanding, unstoppable,
lay a finger to that inflated face
that looks swollen from soaking in water,
the finger endlessly sucked into a hell of flour —
it must be a late snack syndrome.
A sleepwalker's gait, being sucked rippling into the fridge,
a pirate ship, this mouth compensating by nightly plunder.
One night, she devoured a whole chicken all by herself,
can't recall eating it, but in the morning a heap of chicken-bones
on the plate — they, and a flabby belly, the only evidence;
by day, a seamstress sewing cross-stitches in white silk,
by night, a bulimic woman seeking food, hair disheveled,
a smile, a slack smile emerging out of a dark deep-sea depression,
a smile of obesity, ghastly mounds of flesh shifting and rolling,
hating her body, obliged to hate everything in the appetizing world,
wanting to be buried, provoking an impulse to die buried,
the end of the fat woman's fantasy:
being buried.
She wouldn't be able to suggest dying together,
wouldn't be able to die together.
To end in fat burial might be heaven, might be hell.
I want to breathe.
Buried beneath a fat chin, a mountainous swelling bosom,
Mona Lisa, her breath rising laboriously as far as the chin, legs
trembling,
enormous, bulimic, Mona Lisa,
barely breathing, Mona Lisa.

A mother, sitting smiling on a bench at the obesity clinic.

배꽃을 위하여

아스피린, 아달린, 아스피린, 아달린, 막스, 말사스, 마도로스……
아스피린, 아달린, 아스피린, 아달린, 막스, 말사스, 마도로스……
그렇게 속삭이며
배꽃들이 피어나고 있다

아스피린, 아달린, 아스피린, 아달린, 막스, 말사스, 마도로스……
아스피린, 아달린, 아스피린, 아달린, 막스, 말사스, 마도로스……
그렇게 되뇌이며
배꽃들이 달빛 속에 떨어지고 있다

새벽 몇 시인지, 시계의 시침과 분침과 초침 사이
길을 물어도 길이 없고
거실 마루 하얀 배꽃처럼 회푸스레한 빛의 폭포 아래
아버지가 소파에 누워
텔레비젼을 켜놓고 보고 계시는데
아버지, 아버지는 십 년 전에 돌아 가셨잖아요……
시인 고정희가 뱀사골 강물에 빠져 죽던 바로 그 해 봄……
아버지……………

아스피린, 아달린, 아스피린, 아달린, 막스, 말사스, 마도로스……
아스피린, 아달린, 아스피린, 아달린, 막스, 말사스, 마도로스……
정규 프로그램이 끝난 텔레비젼에선
하얀 배꽃 같은 입자들만 방사(放射)될 뿐
형체 없는 브라운관 빛 속에 누워 계시는 아버지

FOR PEAR BLOSSOM

Aspirin, adalin, aspirin, adalin, Marx, Malthus, matroos . . .
Aspirin, adalin, aspirin, adalin, Marx, Malthus, matroos . . .
Whispering this,
pear blossom is blooming.

Aspirin, adalin, aspirin, adalin, Marx, Malthus, matroos . . .
Aspirin, adalin, aspirin, adalin, Marx, Malthus, matroos . . .
Repeating this,
pear blossom is falling in moonlight.

Early dawn, no way to know what time it is,
no way out past hour hand, minute hand, second hand, though I
ask the way.
Under the waterfall of pallid light falling like white pear blossom
on the living-room floor,
father is lying on the sofa
watching the television,
but surely, Father, didn't you die ten years ago . . . ?
The spring of the year the poet Go Jeong-hui fell into the stream in
Baemsa Valley and drowned . . .
Father . . .

Aspirin, adalin, aspirin, adalin, Marx, Malthus, matroos . . .
Aspirin, adalin, aspirin, adalin, Marx, Malthus, matroos . . .
On the television, regular programs finished,
nothing but particles like pear blossom radiate,
Father, lying there in the formless light from the screen . . .

Note: The line "Aspirin, adalin . . ." is a quotation from the story "Wings" by
Yi Sang.

지천명

지천명의 생일 날 저녁이었다

미역을 찾으니 식칼 놓는 자리에 꽂혀 있고
식칼을 찾으니 냉장고 속에 들어 있다
북어가 세탁기 속에서 빙빙 돌아가고
파슬리 양배추 토마토가 장롱 서랍 속에
비누곽 위에 생선이
전자 오븐 레인지 속에 비누가
화분 속에 비타민이
세수 대야 물 속에 소금이

(아, 이렇게 해방이 오고 있구나
세수 대야 물 속에서 녹고 있는 소금을 누가 구원하리?)

핸드폰이 냉동칸 속에서 울리고 있을 때
자꾸만 울리고, 울리고 있을 때

너무나 오래 이름 속에 갇혀 있었다는 것
드디어 내가 내 바깥으로 나갈 줄 알게 되었다는 것,
이 폭소..........
이름의 독재를 가로질러 이 방면(放免)의 풀밭을
날아서, 맨발에 구름과 이슬을 묻히고 이 새로운..........
이 이름 붙일 수 없는.......맨발에 구름을 묻히고서
웃으면서 날아
간다는........

138

FIFTY'S THE AGE WHEN YOU KNOW HEAVEN'S WAYS

It was the evening of my fiftieth birthday.

Looking for seaweed for soup, it was in the place where I keep my
knives;
looking for knives, they had gotten into the fridge.
The dried fish was whizzing round in the washing machine;
parsley, cabbage, tomatoes were in the dresser drawer
fish on the soap dish,
soap in the microwave oven
vitamin pills in a flowerpot
salt in the water in the wash-basin.

(Ah, liberation comes like this, indeed.
Who will save the salt dissolving in the water in the wash-basin?)

As the mobile rings inside the freezer,
just ringing, ringing on and on,

the way I have been for too long imprisoned in my name,
the way I have discovered at last how to get out of myself,
this burst of laughter . . .
crossing beyond a name's despotism, flying
across the meadows of this liberty,
smearing clouds and dew with bare feet, this new . . .
something that cannot be named . . . flying away laughing
after smearing clouds with bare feet,
going . . .

치자 꽃

어딘지 살결에서 죄의 기척이 느껴진다

어느덧 향기는 그렇게 어두운 죄와 의혹 사이에서 나오는 것

천리향 근처에 삼베옷 입은 여인들의 서성임이 있다

GARDENIA FLOWERS

Somewhere on my skin I begin to sense signs of sin.

A fragrance emerging suddenly from between such dark sin and doubt

In the vicinity of that far-spreading fragrance there's a bustling of women in hempen clothes.

여자의 시간

달력 위엔 달이 있고
달걀이 있고
남편 달걀이 태어난 한여름의 사자좌가 있고
시아버지 달걀이 돌아가신 날이 있고
시어머니 달걀이 태어나오신 날도 있고
아, 참, 축 결혼의 날도 있고
노란 국화 근조의 날도 있고
삼대봉사 조모님, 조부님, 증조모님, 증조부님
돌아가신 날들과 태어나신 날들까지도
임신 중독증에 빠진 날들이 있고
산후 우울증의 가위로 머리카락을 마구 잘랐던 날이 있고
친정아버지 돌아가신 날과
친정조부님 조모님 돌아가신 날들도
친정어머니 달걀 태어나신 날이랑
금빛나는 해모수 아들이 나온 날이랑
이름 없는 달걀들이 낙태된 덧없는 날도 있고
빛나는 항공엽서 같은 딸이 나온 날이랑
아이들이 어, 어 ㅁ 마, 첫 말을 건넸던 날이랑
아이들이 드디어 기저귀를 뗐던 역사적 날이랑
딸 달걀의 어여쁜 초경의 날이랑
홍역 같은 사랑의 날 감기 같은 사랑의 날들도

달력을 보면
2900 킬로미터 히말라야 지점 같은
고산증 고독이 몰려오기도 하고
터질 듯한 만원 버스 너무 붐빈다고 생각되기도 하는데
자궁 가족들의 연대기라
일렬횡대, 면면 종대로 이어지며 페밀리 츄리
한 그루
여자의 시간
달이 있고
달걀이 있고
새해 첫날부터 임대가 완료되어 있고
흩어진 피들이 모이고 흩어졌다
다시 모이는

WOMAN'S TIME

Above the calendar there's the moon
and there are eggs,
there's Leo in midsummer when my husband egg was born,
there's the day when father-in-law egg passed away,
there's the day when mother-in-law egg was born,
ah, of course, there's also our happy wedding day
and there are days for yellow chrysanthemums of condolence,
death-days, birthdays of three generations of my husband's
ancestors,
grandmother, grandfather, great-grandmother, great grandfather,
and the day I fell into toxemia during pregnancy,
the day I hacked off my hair with scissors in postpartum
depression,
there's the day when my own father passed away,
the days when my grandfather, grandmother passed away,
there's the day my mother egg was born,
the day mythical Haemosu's son emerged emitting golden rays
and short-lived days when nameless eggs were aborted,
the day our daughter emerged like a glistening airmail postcard,
the day when our children spoke their first word, um-mum-my
the historic day when the children could do without diapers,
the day our daughter egg saw her pretty first menstruation,
days of love like measles, days of love like colds.

When I look at the calendar
I am seized by the solitude of altitude sickness
as if I were high up on the 2,900 km-long Himalayas
and I feel like a bus so overloaded it's about to burst
such are the annals of the uterine family
extending in a single line horizontally or vertically, a "family tree"
a single tree
woman's time
there's the moon
there's an egg
by the first day of the year everything is rented out
while scattered blood gathered then scattered again.
Then gathering again . . .

히딩크 가라사대

거스 히딩크 가라사대

네 어버이를 공경하고
네 이웃을 사랑하라,
살인하지 말고
도둑질하지 말고
간음하지 말고
거짓 증거하지 말고
남의 아내, 비복, 가축 따위 남의 것을 탐내지 말라,
내 이름을 망녕되이 일컫지 말고
내 앞에 다른 우상을 섬기지 말라,

살생하지 말 것이며
탐진치를 버릴 것이며
소망과 믿음과 자비-그 중에서
자비가 없으면 모든 소리가 꽹과리 소리에 지나지 않을 것이며
사군이충(事君以忠)하고   사친이효(事親以孝)하고   교우이신(交友以
信)하고
임전무퇴(臨戰無退)하며
살생유택(殺生有擇)하여
진성보리(眞性菩提), 실지보리(實智菩提), 방편보리(方便菩提)
삼보리를 구하고
부처를 만나면 부처를 죽이고
조사(祖師)를 만나면 조사를 죽이고
견성하라, 자명등(自明燈)하라,
견성하라

우물 안의 개구리들
개골 개골 개골 아멘
개골 개골 개골 나무 관세음.......

144

THUS SPOKE HIDDINK

Thus spoke Gus Hiddink:

Thou shalt honor thy father.
Thou shalt love thy neighbor.
Thou shalt not commit murder.
Thou shalt not steal.
Thou shalt not commit adultery.
Thou shalt not bear false witness.
Thou shalt not covet another's belongings—his wife, his servants,
his cattle, etc.
Thou shalt not take my name in vain.
Thou shalt not serve other idols before me.

Take no life.
Cast off envy, anger, folly.
Hope, faith, love, of these three
without love every voice is merely a clanging cymbal.
Be loyal to the king, pious in serving one's father, trustful toward
friends,
never retreat in battle,
be reluctant to take life,
seek inborn enlightenment, enlightenment through practice,
enlightenment by expedient means,
the three enlightenments.
If you meet Buddha, kill Buddha,
if you meet a patriarch, kill the patriarch
be awakened, be self-enlightened,
be awakened.

Frogs in a well:
croak, croak, croak, Amen.
croak, croak, croak, Namu Gwanseum . . .

히딩크 가라사대

불을 들고 불을 찾는 사람은 누구인가?
밥은 벌써 다 익었는데
"모든 부처는 어디로부터 옵니까?
동산이 물위로 간다."
지금 우리 앞에 서있는 이 이, 에이 맨, 아멘은 누구인가?

거스 히딩크 가라사대
내 앞에서 네 불을 치우고
이제 밥을 먹거라.

Who seeks light while carrying a light?
The rice is already cooked
—where do all buddhas come from?
—the hill is floating off on the water.
Who is this man standing before us? Amen, who is Amen?

Thus spoke Gus Hiddink:
lay aside your light before me
and now eat your rice.

Note: Gus Hiddink served as coach to the Korean soccer team that performed
so well in the 2002 Korea-Japan World Cup. His training methods came
to be seen as recipes for all Korea's problems. "Namu Gwanseum" is a very
popular Buddhist prayer, a phrase repeated many times over.

대형 가라사대

대형 타자기가 머릿속에서 타, 타, 타,
난타하며 타오른다,
(요즈음엔 다 대형을 좋아해요.
대형이 아니면 소비자들도 쳐다보지도 않아요),
대형 타자기는 타, 타, 타,
머릿속에 글자를 난타하며 지나간다,
그 발톱 자국 하나마다 피로 뭉개진 지구가 들려있다.
황폐한 머리, 황폐한 잠, 황폐한 꿈의 육신,
황폐한 성냥이 핏속에서 울고
이 화재는 대형 화재다,
덤불숲이 타오르는 머릿속에서
온몸에 불이 붙어도 도망갈 방법을 추구할 수 없다,

너, 맞지, 너, 신자유주의지, 너 대형이지,
너만 남고 모든 것이 다 사라질 때까지
너는 육체에 타, 타, 타, 타자기를 찍으며
명령한다,
명령을 헤아리기만도 너무 벅차다.
불의 회오리 속에 앉아 타자기를 난타하며
(왜냐하면 그의 이름은 대형이니까)
숙제, 어제의 숙제를 오늘 하고
숙제, 오늘의 숙제를 내일 하는
숙제, 내일의 숙제는 모레, 아니 어느 장구한 세월 뒤에
내 푸른 무덤에 와서나 받아가거라,

이 타, 타, 타, 타자기의
(왜냐하면 그의 이름은 대형이니까)
노예—노예는 언제나 명령 보다 늦게 도착하기 때문에
지각하는 것이고 노예인 것이니
이 대형, 신자유주의는
모든 사람을 타자로, 아니 타자기로, 지각하는 노예로 만들며
(왜냐하면 그의 이름은 대형이니까)
타, 타, 타, 타자기는 달려간다

THUS SPOKE THE LARGE SIZE

The large-size typewriter in my head
pounding away, tap, tap, tap, bursts into flames.
(Nowadays everyone likes the large size.
Unless something's large size, consumers don't look twice.)
The large-size typewriter
passes by, tap, tap, tap, pounding out letters in my head.
In each of those toenail prints the bloody crushed earth is held.
Head laid waste, sleep laid waste, flesh of dreams laid waste,
matches laid waste weep in the blood,
this fire is a large-size fire.
Even if the blazing thickets inside my head,
if my whole body catches fire, I cannot look for a way to escape.

You are, aren't you, you're new liberalism, you're large size,
until everything's vanished and you alone remain
you're giving the orders
while typewriting on the flesh, tap, tap, tap.
It's overwhelming even to count the orders.
Sitting in the whirling flames, pounding at the typewriter
(since its name is large size)
homework, doing yesterday's homework today,
homework, doing today's homework tomorrow,
homework, tomorrow's homework the day after, or after some
lengthy period of time
come to my green grave and collect it.

This tap, tap, tap, typewriter's
(since its name is large size)
slave — is belated, is a slave
because a slave always arrives later than ordered.
So this large-size neoliberalism
turns everyone by type and typewriter into belated slaves,
(since its name is large size)
and tap, tap, tap, the typewriter hurries away.

149

대형 가라사대

거북아, 너는 이제 죽어도 토끼의 간을 가져올 수가 없다
너는 안보이는 대형 타자기에 난타되면서
으깨지면서 죽어 가야만 하든지
아니면 소름끼치도록 대형을 사랑할 수밖에 없다

Turtle, now there's no earthly way you can take out the rabbit's
liver.
You might die crushed, pounded
by an invisible large-size typewriter.

Else all you can do is love the large size till it makes your blood
freeze.

유령 배역

마리아 츠베타예바
실비아 플라스
윤심덕
나혜석
미쳐서 죽은 까미유 끌로델
프리다 칼로

언제나 그들이 더 가까웠다

어디에서부터 무엇이 잘못 되었을까?

비탄에 잠겨 미친 듯이 춤을 추는 지젤

죽을 때까지 춤을 추었을 뿐이다

A CAST OF GHOSTS

Marina Tsvetaeva
Sylvia Plath
Yun Sim-deok
Na Hye-seok
Camille Claudel who died mad
Frida Kahlo

I always felt closer to them.

Where did things start to go wrong?

Giselle, wrapped in grief, dancing like mad,

just danced on and on until she died.

Notes:
° Marina Tsvetaeva (1892–1941) was a Russian and Soviet poet who lived
in exile for many years, returned to the USSR in 1939, experienced great
hardship, and died under suspicious circumstances.
° Yun Sim-deok (1897–1926) was the first Western-style soprano to
become famous in Korea. While studying in Tokyo, she fell in love with a
Korean student, Kim Woo-Jin, who was already married, with a wife and
children living in Korea. They jumped together into the sea on their way
back to Korea.
° Na Hye-seok (1896–1948) was sometimes considered Korea's first
feminist. She was the first Korean woman to paint in Western style, as well
as being a poet and writer. She suffered poverty and discrimination after
an affair with a close friend of her husband led to their divorce in 1930. She
died destitute and alone.

새벽밥

새벽에 너무 어두워
밥솥을 열어 봅니다
하얀 별들이 밥이 되어
으스러져라 껴안고 있습니다
별이 쌀이 될 때까지
쌀이 밥이 될 때까지 살아야 합니다.

그런 사랑 무르익고 있습니다

RICE AT DAWN

At dawn it's so dark
I open the rice-cooker and peer in.
White stars have turned into cooked rice
and are clinging together so tight they might shatter.
I must live on until stars turn into grains of rice,
until rice grains turn into cooked rice.

That kind of love is ripening.

심장딴곳증

인어가 물 밖으로 나와 걸어가는 것처럼
우리가 땅 위를 걸어갈 때
물 밖으로 나와 방울방울 피를 뿌리며 걸어가는 모든 해저의 것들에
대해
안에 있지 못하고 밖으로 쫓겨나올 수밖에 없었던
기막히게 아픈 심장 같은 것에 대하여
나는 노래하고 싶다
심장은 결국 하트 모양이 아니었고
차라리 피투성이 근육 덩어리였다
어딘지 정육의 냄새가 풍겼다,
터널처럼 내 육체는 그만 아픈 심장을 견디다 못해 방출하였고
밖으로 쫓겨 난 심장은
이제 비밀한 단 한 사람조차 숨겨줄 수 없게 되었을 때
구태여 물 밖으로 나와 걸어가는 인어라든가
샤갈의 그림 밖으로 끌려나와 바위에 머리를 박고
여지없이 중력에 추락하는 푸른 신부라든가
머리끝부터 발끝까지 척추를 뚫고 지나간 쇠파이프를 지닌
프리다 칼로의 철철 흘러내리는 피의 성찬식이라든가
그런 어처구니없이 아름다운 것들에 대하여
안에 있지 않고
바깥으로 토해져 나와
아무나 손가락으로 쿡 쿡 찔러보며 아파? 아프겠지?
놀림 받아 정신없이 걷는 심장의 여자라든가
그래도 기도하며 걷는 여자라든가
그래서 불타는 듯 꽃피우며 걷는 여자라든가
맨발이 땅에 닿을 때마다 한 땀 한 땀 핏방울 뜨며 걸어가는
으리으리한 인어 공주,
그런 벙어리, 피의 자수가(刺繡家) 이야기라든가

ECTOPIA CORDIS

When we walk on the dry ground
like mermaids emerging from the water and walking,
I want to sing
about all the submarine creatures that, emerging from the water,
walk sprinkling drops of blood,
about such things as intensely aching hearts unable to stay inside,
driven out.
The heart turned out not to be heart-shaped
but just a bloody lump of muscle.
Somehow it smells like raw meat.
My tunnel-like flesh, unable to stand the aching heart any more,
released it;
once the heart, driven out,
is unable to hide even one secret person,
neither a mermaid that has emerged from the water and is walking,
nor a blue bride falling inevitably under gravity's pull,
drawn out of a Chagall painting, hitting her head on a rock,
nor the blood-soaked eucharist of Frida Kahlo
with that steel pipe that pierced her spine from head to toe,
about such absurdly beautiful things,
nor a woman with a heart that did not stay inside
but came out
and walks in a daze, teased as everyone prods it with a finger,
asking: Is it aching? It must be aching?
nor a woman still praying as she walks,
nor a woman walking blossoming with flowers as if on fire
nor a stately mermaid princess
walking along, leaving one stitch of blood each time her bare feet
touch the ground,
nor tales about such mute embroiderers of blood.

나는 반죽 중

이것은 참회도 아니고 고백도 아니다,
그저 불안의 자서전........
나는 언제나 반죽 중이었고,
어디에 나는 있었을까,
언제 나는 있었을까,
언제나 반죽 중인 진흙이
물을 향해 가고 있거나
자기를 구워줄 불을 향해 가고 있거나
어느 때는 먼지, 어느 때는 연기, 어느 때는 향기의 오른팔,
메마르고 견고한 명사를 사모해 아래로 가고 있거나
가끔은 천상을 향해....
그런 저런 과정 중에 나라는 것을 얼핏 만나기도 했지만
황토를 향해 무작정 허물어지고 있는 몸통,
나비 날개가 설핏 돋아나고 있는 어깨,
중언부언, 뭐 그런 등등......의 어느 과정 속에
무지개에 머리를 감고 있는 나를 만나는 날도
눈썹 위에 지옥 불을 피워놓고 있는 날도,
풍선이 둥둥,
너는 너무 단단해,
너는 너무 물렁해,
너는 너무, 너무, 너무......나도 종잡을 수가 없어,
너로 불리우는 나, 나는 단지 하나의 명사,
그 고유명사에 매달려 거미줄을 짓고 있는 음산한 거미,
나는 나다, 나는 내가 아니다,
될 수도 없고 그런 것은 애초에 없었다,
밀가루 반죽을 코에 묻히거나
시멘트 반죽에 흙곽을 담그거나
뭐, 그저 그런, 과정 중에서
풍선은 둥둥
우리는 스쳐감이었고조립된 것은 반드시 멸하기 마련이고,
사랑도 미움도 그렇게 애초에 책임을 질 수가 없는

BEING KNEADED

This is neither repentance nor confession,
merely an autobiography of anxiety . . .
I was always being kneaded.
I wonder where I was,
I wonder when I was,
the clay being kneaded all the time
is heading for water or
heading for the fire that will bake it,
sometimes dust, sometimes smoke, or the right arm of fragrance,
or heading downward, yearning for a parched, solid noun,
or sometimes heading for the sky . . .
in the course of this and that I chanced to meet myself
but the body collapsing blindly heading for waste ground,
shoulders with butterfly wings emerging slightly,
over and over, so on and so forth . . . that kind of process
days when I meet myself washing my hair in a rainbow,
days when I set hellfire burning on my eyebrows,
balloons floating aloft,
you're too hard,
you're too soft,
you're too, too, too . . . I too can't get the gist,
this "I" known as "you," I'm just a mere noun,
a somber spider spinning a web hitched to that proper noun,
I'm I, I'm not myself,
can't become it, such a thing never existed from the start.
Smearing wheat dough over my nose,
or immersing my breast into a slurry of cement,
why, like that, in that kind of process
we were something brushing past,
balloons floating aloft,
while assembled things were bound to fall apart,
and ephemeral I, unable from the start to take responsibility
for things like love or hate, encountered you in that kind of
process,

나는 반죽 중

덧없는 내가 당신을 어느 과정에서 만났고
스쳤고,
십자가 위에서 모든 살과 피의 반죽이 다 쏟아져 내렸듯
반죽 중에 있는 진흙과 물이 얼떨결에 합쳐져
큰 바다에 다 녹아 흩어질 참 검소한 반죽.......

Being kneaded

and just brushed past,
as if a dough made up of blood and flesh were cascading down
from the cross,
clay and water being kneaded together, combined in confusion,
a truly frugal dough of salt, all bound to melt into one vast ocean . . .

스티그마타

두 손과 두 발에 못 박히고 옆구리에서부터 심장까지 긴 창으로
찔렸다
그 흘러내리는 다섯 자리 피 안에서
얼마나 많은 사람들이 태어나고 있는가

그 고통 보다 큰 사랑은 없고
그 못 자국 보다 넓은 우주는 없다

STIGMATA

Nails were hammered into hands and feet,
then he was pierced to the heart by a spear in his side.
So many people are being born
in the blood flowing down from those five wounds.

No love is greater than that agony,
no cosmos is vaster than the print of those nails.

미제레레

성 금요일 밤
모든 촛불이 하나하나 꺼진다
어둠 속에 남겨지는 사람들은
모두 홀로 어둠 속에 남겨지는 사람이다
어둠 속에 남겨진 사람들은
모두 홀로 무릎 꿇고 남겨진 사람이다
그가 꺾으신 뼈로 즐거워하*며
피아니시모
한 목소리가 모두의 목소리로
미제레레 메이
이런 밤에
그 분의 수난을 생각하는 사람들은
모두 홀로 그 수난이 된 사람이다
죄에서 시작하여 사랑과 긍휼과 자비를 구하는 사람들은
모두 홀로 사랑과 자비와 긍휼이 필요한 사람이다
모두 목소리가 한 목소리로
한 목소리가 모두 목소리로
피아니시모
미제레레 메이
그가 꺾으신 뼈로 즐거워하*며
팔레스트리나, 나니노, 알레그리........
제사는 상한 심령의 입술로

* 다윗의 <시편 51> 중에서

164

MISERERE

On Good Friday evening
all the candles are put out, one after another.
The people left in the dark
are people all left alone in the dark.
The people left in the dark
are people all left kneeling alone.
"Let the bones you have broken rejoice"
pianissimo
one voice as the voice of all:
Miserere mei.
On such a night
the people pondering his Passion
are people all alone becoming that Passion.
The people who start in sin and plead for love, compassion, mercy,
are all people in need of love, mercy, compassion.
The voices of all as one voice,
one voice as the voice of all,
pianissimo:
Miserere mei.
"Let the bones you have broken rejoice."
Palestrina, Nanino, Allegri . . .
a sacrifice from the lips of a broken spirit.

Note: "Miserere mei, Deus" are the opening words of Psalm 51, "Have mercy on me, God." The renaissance Italian composer Gregorio Allegri (1582–1652), set the words to music. The poet heard a recording of Allegri's Miserere, was moved by it and wrote her poem on the basis of the accompanying notes. She is not a Catholic and has never seen a celebration of the service of Tenebrae, where the Miserere was originally sung. She expresses her own (Protestant) faith in God's mercy toward human suffering·

반투명한 불투명

그런 건가? 보이지 않는 건가?
그런 건가? 들리지 않는 건가?
그런 건가? 알지 못하는 건가?
그런 건가? 다 소용없는 건가?
그런 건가? 해가 또 지는 건가?
그런 건가? 이렇게 살다 가라는 건가?
그런 건가? 하루하루 오늘은 괴로움의 나열인데
그런 건가? 띄어쓰기도 없이 밀려오는 나날
그런 건가? 내일도 오늘과 같다는 건가?

TRANSLUCENT OPACITY

Is that how it is? Is it invisible?
Is that how it is? Is it inaudible?
Is that how it is? Is it unknowable?
Is that how it is? Is it all pointless?
Is that how it is? Is the sun setting again?
Is that how it is? Being obliged to live like this then go?
Is that how it is? Day after day, each today is an array of anguish.
Is that how it is? Days that come thronging without any pause.
Is that how it is? Will tomorrow turn out just like today?

입춘대길

닭들은 항상 새끼들과 함께 다닌다,
가모장제인 모양이다,
아빠는 어디 갔나? 아직도 퇴원을 안했나?
웬일인지 두 진영이 개나리 꽃 아래서 싸우고 있다
강, 강, 호르르르......
강, 강, 호르르르.......

잡아 뜯겨진 깃털들이 노오란 꽃밭에 휘몰아쳐
오늘, 거기는,
미친 듯이 환한 꽃잎 중심 천지.........
싸우지 말고 카르페 디엠 하라! 하려는데
이 닭들이 때렸다! 맞았다! 때렸다! 맞았다! 호루루루 엎어지면서
강, 강, 호르르르......카르페 디엠!

GOOD LUCK FOR THE COMING SPRING

Hens are always accompanied by their chicks.
It looks like a matriarchy.
Where's Dad? Not out of hospital yet?
For some reason two sides are fighting beneath the forsythia.
Bang, bang, grrrr . . .
Bang, bang, grrrr . . .

Torn-out feathers go swirling round the yellow flower patch,
today, there,
a world centered on madly bright petals . . .
I try to tell them not to fight, rather "Carpe diem!"
These hens: Hit! Struck! Hit! Struck! Grrrrr, toppling
Bang, bang, grrrr . . . "Carpe diem!"

제4인칭의 꿈

나
너
그
그녀
모든 것
그 모든 것
그것이 아닌 것
그 모든 것이 끝난 곳
그 모든 것이 시작된 곳
다시 돌아가
아버지의 잘려진 남근이 던져진 거품 속에서
비너스가 태어난 곳
오렌지 혹은 레몬의 잼 마아멀레이드
그녀의 여근곡에 푸른 파도 거품 꽃피던 곳
태어나 처음 던진 말 아, 아, 아, 아, 아,……그
순결한 모음 가득찬 곳
그 첫 음성 들끓는 곳
그 모든 것이 다 끝난 곳
그 모든 것이 또 시작하는 곳
그녀
그
너
나

DREAM OF A FOURTH PERSON PRONOUN

I
you
he
she
everything
all those things
something that's none of those
the place where all those things end
the place where all those things begin
going back again
the place where Venus was born
out of the foam where her father's severed penis was hurled
orange or lemon jam, marmalade,
the place where foam from blue waves blossomed in her secret
valley
the first word pronounced after being born : a, a, a, a, a, . . . the
place full of those pure vowels
the place where that first sound bubbles up
the place where all those things end completely
the place where all those things begin again
she
he
you
I

무지개 고개

여기가 어디야?
왜 이리 찬란해?
이 향기는 뭐야? 비 내린 뒤 쟈스민 냄새 같애,
당신은 뭐해? 또 자는 거야?
아니, 아직, 아직.......
아 참 당신은 아프지.......
너는 어딨어? 왜 안들어와?
딸이 이렇게 늦게 다니다니, 원, 참, 말세야, 말세.....
엄마 나 뉴욕에 있잖아, 콜롬비아 대학원에
유학 왔잖아,
아, 참, 그렇지, 그래, 맞다, 맞아, 너, 유학 갔지,
그런데 이 놈은 왜 아직 안들어와?
한국 남자 대학생들이란 참, 서울은 음주에 젖어,
뭐야? 엄마, 나 지금 군대 왔잖아,
입대했잖아,
아, 그래, 너, 참, 군대갔니?
당신이 편하게 잠들 수 있는 것은 우리의 아들들이
일선에서 조국을 지키고 있기 때문입니다,
그래, 어딘가 밤이 수상하고
내 머리가 수상하고
별빛도 수상하고
무언가 찬란한 빛 가운데 무지개 다리 같은 것이
지상에서부터 하늘까지 막 퍼져 올라가는 느낌인데

여보세요! 네? 누구세요?
어디세요? 네? 어디시라고요?
어디요?
잘못 거셨어요!

RAINBOW PASS

Where am I?
Why is it so dazzlingly bright?
What's this smell? It's like the smell of jasmine after rain.
What are you doing? Still asleep?
No, not yet, not yet . . .
Ah, right, you're sick . . .
Where are you now? Why aren't you home?
What kind of a daughter are you, hanging out this late? What a
hopeless world, hopeless . . .
But Mom, I'm in New York, studying
at Columbia University Graduate School, aren't I?
Ah, right, of course, right, sure, you're studying abroad, of course,
but why's he not home yet?
Korean college students, these guys, well, Seoul's soaking in booze.
What? Mom, I'm doing my military service, aren't I?
I've been drafted into the army.
Ah, right, of course, your military service.
The reason we're able to sleep soundly, not worrying, is because
our sons are up on the front line guarding the nation.
Right, somehow the evening's suspicious
my head's suspicious
and the starlight's suspicious.
It's like feeling that some kind of rainbow bridge is rising up from
the earth
in the midst of dazzling bright light and spreading out over the sky.

Hello! Yes? Who is this?
Who? What? Who did you say you were?
Who?
You've dialed the wrong number!

173

무지개 후회

달걀이 부화되기를
그렇게 기다리고 있었는데
무지개가 달걀을 가져가 버렸네,
그렇게 기다리고 있었는데
비가 너무 많이 내린 거지,

무지개는 나에게 많은 것을 주었으나
언제부터인가, 주기 보다는 가져가는 것이 더 많아졌네
빗 속에서 무지개를 생각하지 말아,
달걀이 둥둥 다 떠내려 갔잖아,
비 그친 후부터
무지개를 그냥 보면 되는데

너무 많은 무지개 꿈을 꾸었어,
비에 달걀이 다 휩쓸려 가는데도
꿈을 꾸었지, 그것만,
세상에 비 그친 후 솟는 무지개는
다 내 피와 헌신으로 솟은 것을 알아줘,

무지개야, 그래서 네가 가져가는 것이 너무 많아,
그래도 얼굴에 두 눈썹을 봐,
무지개를 꼭 잡으려고
내가 붙든 우듬지,
칠색 무지개가 심고 간 검은 절망이야
그래도 약속해 줘,
나는 다시 또 달걀들을 낳을께

RAINBOW REGRETS

I was waiting so eagerly
for an egg to hatch
but a rainbow took the egg away.
I was waiting so eagerly.
It's because it had been raining far too much

The rainbow gave me many things but
from a certain moment, it took away rather more than it gave.
Never think of a rainbow in the rain.
Weren't the eggs all carried away?
Once it's stopped raining
just looking up at the rainbow will do.

I dreamed too many rainbow dreams
though the eggs were swept away in the rain.
I dreamed only that one dream.
Please, acknowledge that the rainbow which emerged
over the world after the rain stopped
sprang up because of my blood and devotion

Rainbow! You take far too many things away,
but look at the two eyebrows on my face,
the tree top I'm holding on to,
intending to catch the rainbow for sure,
a black despair, planted by the departing rainbow,
but promise me
I'll lay some more eggs.

바람을 옷에 싼 여자

여자,
바람을 옷으로 싸고
물을 보자기로 모으는 여자,
해와 별을 가슴에 기르고
정액과 피를 모아
(아, 너로구나, 너였구나....)
그것은 바람의 연애, 사람을 태어나게 한 여자

두 손으로 바람을 모아
뼈와 근육과 신경과 골수를 짜넣은 여자
영혼을 살로 싼 여자
심장 속에 절대로 꺼지지 않는 불을 넣은 여자
언제나 위험 보다 더 위험하고
허무 보다 더 허무하고
시간 보다 더 덧없는 여자

두 손에 모은 바람은 흐터지고
보자기로 싼 물은 흘러 떨어지고
살에 새겨 넣은 혼은 날아가고
숨결로 구름을 만들어도
절대로 꺼지지 않는 불을 심장 속에 간직한
이 여자, 인류 대대로 바람을 옷으로 싼 여자,
불 붙는 초가삼간, 인간을 탄금(彈琴)하는 여자

The Woman Who Wrapped the Wind in Clothes

A woman,
a woman who wraps the wind in clothes
and binds up water in a cloth,
nursing sun and stars at her breast,
gathering together sperm and blood
(ah, so you did it, it was you . . .)
that was the wind's love, that woman who brought someone to
birth

A woman who, gathering the wind with both hands,
weaves together bone and muscle, nerves and marrow,
a woman who wraps the soul in flesh,
a woman who sets in the heart a flame that should never go out,
a woman who is always more dangerous than danger,
more empty than emptiness,
more fleeting than time.

The wind gathered by both hands scattered
the water bound in a cloth flowed away
the soul enclosed in flesh flew off
though she made clouds of breath
this woman who cherishes in her heart
a flame that should never go out,
a woman who has, generation after generation,
wrapped the wind in clothes,
a cottage aflame, a woman who plucks on human strings.

여자가 낳은 것

여자가 낳은 것마다
물이 되어버리고
여자가 낳은 것마다 바람이 되어버리니
그럼 여자는 물을 낳은 것인가, 바람을 낳은 것인가
여자가 낳은 것은 뼈이고 흙일 뿐인가

바람의 어머니
물의 어머니
뼈의 어머니
흙의 어머니

보아라, 순간에서 순간까지
이슬에서 이슬까지
여자가 낳은 것이 하늘 아래 가장 좋은 것이면서
여자가 낳은 것이
또 하늘 아래 가장 아픈 것

WHAT A WOMAN GIVES BIRTH TO

Everything a woman gives birth to
turns into water.
Everything a woman gives birth to turns into wind.
So does a woman give birth to water or wind?
Is what a woman gives birth to nothing more than bones and clay?

Wind's mother
water's mother
bones' mother
clay's mother

Behold, from moment to moment
from dew to dew
what a woman gives birth to is the most precious thing in the world
and what a woman gives birth to
is also the most painful thing in the world.

사랑

사랑은 현찰이 아닌겨,
그래도 든든한겨.......

가난한 어머니가 가난한 아들에게 말했다

가난한 아들은 그 말조차 싫었다
사랑만 아니라면 어떤 짓이든 할 수 있는데

현찰을 못주는 어머니는 가난한 아들에게 못내 미안한 마음이었다
사랑은 더듬더듬 말을 더듬는겨......

아들은 사랑이 어서 현찰이 되기를 바라는 마음 뿐이었다

가난한 어머니 당뇨 발이 굽어들고 있었다

LOVE

Love is not money,
still, it makes you feel secure . . .

So said a poor mother to her poor son.

That poor son hated the word.
So long as it wasn't love, he could do anything.

Unable to give him money, the mother felt most apologetic.
Love always fumbles . . . fumbles . . . for words . . .

The son's heart was full of a hope that love would turn into money
soon.

His poor mother's feet were being twisted by diabetes.

행복 선언

다른 것은 없다,
바보니까, 행복하자

DECLARATION OF HAPPINESS

There's nothing else.
We're foolish, so let's be happy.

수평선

이름 석 자 다 귀찮다
서있는 것도 귀찮다

그저 저 수평선이나 되었으면

HORIZON

The three characters forming my name are all a nuisance.
Standing's a nuisance, too.

I just wish I could become the horizon.

나와 너

나는 때때로 내가 아닐지도 모른다,
네가 거기 있을 때만
나는 나일 수 있는지도 모른다,
신문 글자나 잡지 사진을 전사한 뒤
그 위에 거친 붓질,
희미하게 서로 돋아나는 아련한 포개짐,
아크릴 염료의 화려함, 식물염료의 은은함,

내가 네가 되고
네가 내가 되고
로버트 라우센버그 작품을 보면
길거리에서 주운 신문, 화장지, 헝겊, 흙, 잎사귀들도
서로 서로 네가 될 수 있는 것같다,
타이어에 염소 박제를 콤바인하고
피라미드에 낙타를 콤바인하고
회화,조각, 사진, 판화를 콤바인하고
추상 표현주의, 네오 다다, 팝 아트, 실크 스크린 프린팅을
콤바인하고
일상 풍경이 환상이 되는
실크에 신문 잡지 사진을 콜라쥬로 붙인 모니터

해라, 해라, 콤바인해라,
평면과 입체를 불문하고 콤바인해라,
시대의 명제는, 자화상의 명제는 콤바인이다-
회화와 조각만이 아니고
서로 서로 헤어져 있는 것들
콤바인해라, 손을 잡고
어제 싸우던 것들도 콤바인을 하면 그럴 듯하다,
너와 내가 세상에 자취도 없이 사라질 때
우리는 무덤 속 그것이 되어
그것으로
그것만큼 존재하면서
마지막 작품 흙과 콤바인하기로

I AND YOU

I may sometimes not be myself.
It's almost as if I can be myself
only when you're there.
After copying newsprint or photos from magazines
the brush strokes over them,
the hazy overlappings by which they make one another faintly grow,
the garishness of acrylic dyes, the mellowness of food colorings

I turn into you
you turn into me.
When I glimpse a work by Robert Rauschenberg
it seems that scattered newspapers, tissues, scraps of cloth, clay,
leaves, picked up in the street,
each and all can turn into you,
tires combine with stuffed goats
pyramids combine with camels
paintings, sculptures, photos, prints combine
abstract expressionism, neo-dada, pop art, silk screen prints combine
a monitor made into a collage with newsprint and magazine photos
stuck to silk
where an ordinary landscape turns into an illusion.

Go on, do it, combine!
Ignore planes and solids, combine.
The proposition of the age, the proposition of self-portraiture is to
combine
not only painting and sculpture,
even things scattered far apart
combine, join hands.
If things that yesterday were fighting combine, they'll look quite good.
When you and I vanish without trace from the world
we'll become just that in the grave
and as such
will exist to that extent,
a final work, intent on combining with the earth.

우리가 자궁 안에 두고온 것들

출발했지, 얼굴에
온 피 묻히고
만세를 부르며
그렇게 나왔지,
아무 것도 가지고 올 수 없어 빈손으로
울며 불며 그렇게 나왔지,

피의 보자기가 찢어지고
물의 보자기가 찢어지고
처음 보는 큰 가위가 다가와
아름다운 다리 사이 계곡으로 쏟아져 나왔지,
어쩔 수 없이, 너무 큰 하늘,
어쩔 수 없이, 너무 많은 빛,
어쩔 수 없이, 엉덩이에 푸른 반점

그렇게 나왔지,
내동댕이쳐져서 다 두고 나왔지,
무엇을 다 두고
몸만 나왔는데,
한평생 생각해도 다 그리워 못하고
돌아가서 다시 알아봐야지

THE THINGS WE LEFT BEHIND IN THE WOMB

We set off, our faces
covered with blood,
cheering like mad
that's how we emerged,
unable to bring anything with us, empty-handed
crying, shouting, that's how we emerged

The wrapping of blood was torn,
the wrapping of water was torn,
huge forceps approached, never seen before,
we burst out into the valley between a lovely pair of legs.
Inevitably, too vast a sky,
inevitably, too much light,
inevitably, the blue birthmark on the bottom.

That's how we emerged.
Thrown out, leaving everything behind, we emerged.
Leaving something behind,
we emerged with only our bodies.
A whole lifetime of yearning's not been enough,
we should go back and check.

앵무새 기르기

앵무새는 더 많은 앵무새가 퍼지기를 원하였다,
천지가 앵무새 나라가 되기를 원하였다,
앵무새는 앵무새 알을 사방에 퍼뜨려
앵무새 국토가 커지기를 바랬다,
앵무새는 앵무새의 권력을 사랑하였다

학교로 갔다,
앵무새 알을 퍼뜨리기에 가장 좋은 장소였다,
유치원과 초등학교는 그러나 어려운 장소다,
그들의 머리에는 앵무새 노래에 대한 의심이 있고,
앵무새 노래를 뛰어넘는 활력이 있고,
자기 노래를 부르고자 하는 벅찬 기개가 있지만
크게 걱정할 것은 없었다,
머리를 깎고 중, 고등학교를 다니는 동안
그들도 곧 깨우치게 될 터였다,
앵무새 기르기에 편입되지 않는 한
살 길은 없다는 것을,

앵무새는 더 많은 앵무새가 동참하기를 원하였다,
누가 주인 앵무새인지,
누가 노예 앵무새인지
복사가 복사를 낳아 구분은 희미해져 가고
남은 것은 앵무새 권력과 앵무새들의 합창,
그 합창에서 빠지면 죽는 길 밖에 없다는 것을
누구나 다 알게 되는 것이다,
추락하는 것에는 손이 없기 때문이다
국가의 앵무새야,
제국의 앵무새야,
앵무새 죽이기라는 책도 있지만
(국가가 누구지? 제국은 또 누구?)
지금 장려되는 사업은 앵무새 기르기,
앵무새 기르기만 번쩍번쩍 성업 중,
그대 목소리, 그대 노래는 밥풀 하나 들지 못하리

PARROT BREEDING

One parrot wanted to propagate a lot more parrots.
It wanted the whole world to become a nation of parrots.
The parrot hoped to make the realm larger
by propagating parrot eggs everywhere.
That parrot loved parrot-power.

It went to the schools.
They were the best places to propagate parrot eggs.
But kindergarten and elementary schools are difficult places.
In their heads they have doubts about parrots' songs,
they have more vitality than parrots' songs,
they have tremendous courage, intent on singing their own songs
but still there was no need to worry about them too much.
Once they began to attend middle and high school with their hair
cut short
they would surely come to realize
that unless they were incorporated into parrot breeding
they would have no way of living.

The parrot wanted a lot more parrots to join in.
Which was boss parrot?
Which was slave parrot?
As clone gave birth to clone the distinction grew hazy.
What remained was parrot-power and parrot-chorus.
Everyone would come to know that dropping out of that chorus
left no option but death,
because without a helping hand you're bound to fall.
Nation's parrots!
Empire's parrots!
There's also a book titled "Killing Parrots" but
(what is a nation? and what is an empire?)
what's being promoted now is parrot breeding,
parrot breeding alone is a brilliantly thriving business.
Your voice, your songs are not worth a jot.

191

사랑 3
　　— 고엽제 이야기

나르키서스는 자신만을 사랑하는 남자
에코는 그만을 사랑하는 여자

그가 말한다
왜 너는 나를 사랑하는 거야?
에코는 따라서 말한다
나를 사랑해줘요.

그가 말한다
제발 나에게 가까이 오지 말아!
그녀는 말한다
가까이 오세요!

나르키서스는 자기 말을 할 줄 아는 남자
에코는 그의 말을 (잘못) 따라 하는 여자

모든 사랑에는 혀의 고엽제가 들어 있다
혀를 말리는 하얀 약이 키스할 때마다 배급된다

Love 3
—A tale of defoliants

Narcissus: a man who loves only himself.
Echo: a woman who loves only him.

He says:
Why do you love me?
Echo repeats:
Love me.

He says:
Please don't come near me!
She says:
Come near me!

Narcissus: a man who knows what he means.
Echo: a woman who (mistakenly) repeats what he says.

Every love contains the tongue's defoliant.
A liquid that makes the tongue curl up accompanies each kiss.

한국식 죽음

*김금동씨 (서울 지방검찰청 검사장), 김금수씨 (서울 초대병원
병원장), 김금남씨 (새한일보 정치부 차장) 부친상, 박영수씨 (
오성물산 상무이사) 빙부상 – 김금연씨 (세화여대 가정과 교수)
부친상, 지상옥씨 (삼성대학 정치과 교수) 빙부상, 이제이슨씨 (재미,
사업)빙부상=7일 상오 하오 3시 10분 신촌 세브란스 병원서 발인
상오 9시 364-8752 장지 선산

그런데 누가 죽었다고?

DEATH KOREAN-STYLE

* The death is announced of the father of Mr. Kim Geum-Dong (Chief Prosecutor, Seoul District Public Prosecutor's Office), Mr. Kim Geum-Su (Director, Seoul First Hospital), Mr. Kim Geum-Nam (Deputy head reporter, Political Desk, Saehan Daily), father-in-law of Mr. Pak Yeong-su (Managing Director, Oseong Corporation), the father of Kim Geum-Yeon (Professor, Home Management Department, Sehwa Women's University), father-in-law of Ji Sang-Ok (Professor, Political Science Department, Samseong University) and of Jason Lee (Business, U.S.). On the 7th of this month at 3:10 a.m. in Sinchon Severance Hospital. Funeral departs 9:00 a.m. for the family burial ground. Contact: 364-8752

But who does it say has died?

한국식 실종자

• 부음

◆ 이상준(골드라인 통상 대표), 오회용(국제 가정의학 원장), 손회준(남한 방송국), 김문수(동서대학 교수)씨 빙모상= 4일 오후 삼성 서울 병원. 발인 6일 오전 5시.

누군가 실종되었음이 분명하다

다섯 명씩이나!

순교 문화의 품위를 지키면서
손수건으로 입을 막고 다소곳이

남근 신의 가족 로망스 이야기

MISSING PERSONS, KOREAN-STYLE

• Obituary

◆ The beloved mother-in-law of Lee Sang-Jun (President, Goldline Trading), O Hee-Yong (Director, International Family Clinic), Son Hee-Jun (Namhan Broadcasting), Kim Mun-Su (Professor, Dongseo University). At 4:00 p.m. at Seoul Samseong Hospital. Funeral departs on the 6th at 5:00 a.m.

It should be obvious that several names are missing here.

Five of them, in all!

The women, quietly gagged with handkerchiefs,
upholding the dignity of our Martyrdom Culture.

The romantic story of a phallic god's family.

Note: These last two poems are satiric parodies of Korean death announcements in which by convention the names of women are not indicated if at all possible, the women being represented by their husbands' names even when their own (nameless) mother has died.

CORNELL EAST ASIA SERIES

CORNELL
East Asia Series

Order online at www.einaudi.cornell.edu/eastasia/publications

.